A Queen of Dreams Quintessential Guide

Must Be Present To Win

How To Get Out Of The Ditch & Plug Back In To Your Passion

Tina Ferguson

Chance Allen Publishing
P.O. Box 864093
Plano, Texas 75086

First Published in 2010 by Chance Allen Publishing

Publisher's Note: Neither the publisher nor the author is engaged in rendering professional advice or services to the individual reader. The ideas, procedures and suggestions contained in this book are not intended as a substitute for consulting with a professional. All matters regarding your health and mental well-being require medical supervision. Neither the author nor the publisher shall be liable or responsible for any loss or damage allegedly arising from any information or suggestion in this book.

ISBN 978-0-9817390-1-4

Printed in the United States of America

Cover Design Michelle Preast www.MichellePreast.com
Copy Editor Maria Smith www.TheWordSmithGroup.com

All stories in this book are true. Clients have consented to share their stories, and in some instances, details have been compiled or omitted to protect the privacy and intimate nature of client breakthroughs.

Praise for Tina Ferguson and Her Breakthrough Programs...

"In the past three months of working with Tina both my personal energy and my business success have sky rocketed to new levels. I have done other similar type of work with coaches but never have my own understanding and vision come together so quickly and powerfully. I know what I need to do and am committed to doing it. Working with Tina is like taking the Concorde, the fast track to where you want to be. Get ready to enjoy the ride."

–Minette Riordan, Ph.D., President, Scissortail Publishing www.MinetteRiordan.com

"Something clicked when I heard you speak. I think that something was *me*. All at once, it was apparent. What *am* I waiting on? This was the clarity I asked for. Thank you!"

–Workshop Participant

"My experience with the Hearts of Fire Retreat and Tina and Mark was transformational and miraculous! I rediscovered parts of myself I had hidden away for a long time. It was the kind of insight and movement that would take *years* to accomplish ordinarily. Tina delivers BIG! There are really no words to describe such internal growth in such a short period. The information affected me on all levels and I would recommend this program to anyone who wants to grow/prosper/love bigger/live a fuller more stress free life/not live in pain anymore; and who wants to participate FULLY in life!"

–Dorine Fernandez, Founder, Golden Lotus Transformational Health Center
www.GoldenLotusTransformationalHealthCenter.com

"This morning I listened to your radio show about plugging into your magic. At one point in the audio, you talked about manifesting your intentions and said that if they aren't manifesting what you are asking for, there's a reason. Well, I haven't sold over the phone in a long time so instantly I realized that was my biggest block. As my day went along I felt restless and realized I needed to take a break and do the forgiveness exercises you suggested. While in the middle of the meditation, my grandfather and I came up as two people who needed forgiveness. I did the energy work, cleared that block and moved on to the next thing that came up which was clearing the fear of "answering questions over the phone" when the UNTHINKABLE happened…the phone rang. I took the call. My voice was shaky, but I was crystal clear about how I could help this man's firm and gave a ton of examples. At the end of our conversation he said, "Perfect Brandon, I want to weave your services into my firm." Well, I'm proud to say that I've gotten over the fear of taking calls and giving examples. My business continues to grow. Next time, I won't blow it off when you say on your show, 'People, you ask and the answer is given, maybe not how you want to hear it, but God and the Messenger's will *always* answer.' Thank you so much."

–Brandon Landry, Vice President, Client Services, The Client Getter www.TheClientGetter.com

"If you want to be the leader that you were born to be, to act on your inner voice, to grow your business and be the success you know you can be, work with Tina. She has been an amazing guide in aligning my business with my personal desires and talents. She knows how to get to the heart of the matter, assist you to overcome blocks and move forward very quickly. Your investment will be returned many times over. Tina continues to hold me up to the vision we created together and offers ongoing support and resources that inspire me and keep me moving in inspired action."

–Kathy Garland, Transformational Leader www.KathyGarland.com

"How does it feel to know you have completely changed the course of a life? How does it feel to hear you have completely changed the course of MANY lives? What greater gift is there than to show people where they are, show them who they REALLY are and to give hope by assisting in reconnecting their true selves with their current being? Thank you does not seem to be enough, but, thank you."

–Susan Tate, Award-winning Designer & Artist

"From the moment I set the intention to work with Tina Ferguson this past summer, things began to move for me. In our first session together, I had some aha moments and began having breakthroughs, which propelled my business forward very fast. I was able to make decisions that positively impacted my business, including revamping, repartnering and relocating. My first week in her program, I quadrupled my business, and it has continued to grow steadily this year. Tina has helped me to grow both as an individual and as a business woman, and I am benefiting greatly from her guidance. Working with Tina this year, I have been able to fill in the missing pieces to doing work that I love and being successful and fulfilled. Tina will take you on the fast track if you are ready for it, and she will challenge you in great ways to create and live your best life."

–Michelle Barr, M.Ed., Holistic Coach, Energy Medicine Intuitive, Speaker, Author & Radio Host www.MichelleBarr.com

"I have been coaching with Tina Ferguson for less than a year and signed up for her new group coaching a month ago. I have seen major changes both personally and professionally since becoming her coaching client. Despite several unsuccessful attempts to move out of the day-to-day operations in my business, since working with Tina I have successfully done so and have watched my team take off on their own. Sales have increased 15 percent in one month with a new major client in the works. I have also taken action on my life's passion–music–and am watching everything align with ease. Tina has amazing talent for seeing the truth in her clients and helping them realize their true potential!"

–Doreen Fisher, President, Rainbow Outsourcing www.RainbowOutsourcing.com & www.DoeFisher.com

Also By Tina Ferguson

The Power of Love

The Power of Love Meditations

The Power of Love: Spiritual Power Tools for Living

The Marketing Multiplier Effect: Making Money is So Easy, You Can Do This Too!

A Queen of Dreams Quintessential Guide

Must Be Present to Win

How To Get Out Of The Ditch & Plug Back In To Your Passion

First Edition

Tina Ferguson, a.k.a. The Queen of Dreams

"Today you are You,
that is truer than true.
There is no one alive who
is Youer than You."
–Theodor Seuss Geisel, a.k.a. Dr.Seuss

Dedicated to. . .

Jesus, Ricah and Alliseah
who invited me to rest in the ditch
when I thought I had lost my way.

I love you all so much
there are no words.

Thank you for always
being there for me.

I'll do my best to
share true love with others.

This book is another step toward
sharing what you've taught me
about unconditional love.

Acknowledgments

The acknowledgments section is one of my favorites in every book I read. I love to peek into an author's life and meet the people who have helped to bring his or her work into the world. I am grateful to have so many people who support me and love me each and every day.

Home Heart Team

Mark Ferguson, a.k.a. The King of Hearts, a.k.a. Mr. Tina Ferguson, a.k.a. The Guy Who Knows Everything, a.k.a. Disco, you are my rock and my soft place to land. Ten years ago when I asked God to send the right guy, little did I know how right Mr. Right would turn out to be. You bring new appreciation to the words unconditional love. I love that you love seeing the Truth in people as much as I do. Thank you for always being a dream believer for me and seeing the Truth in me. I love you so very much.

Chance Ferguson, a.k.a. Mr. Sunshine, you bring new meaning to living life out loud. I love that you chose me to be your mom. You are truly the miracle dad and I never thought we would experience. You've invited us to play, laugh and dance in your own special way, and have taught us so much about having fun. My life and work wouldn't be nearly as vibrant without you. I love you.

Rico Ferguson, a.k.a. the Gentle Giant. What a big heart you have. I felt a call from deep within my soul that it was time to add a puppy to our house. You are our forever dog, and we are so grateful for your sweet, sweet nature. Who could imagine that 190 lbs. of canine love could be so much fun? You are truly just like us–super sensitive with a big heart for everyone you meet.

Carolyn Badaracco, a.k.a. Nana, thank you for being what friends call, "my second wife." If it takes a village to raise a child, you are a very large part of that village. Mark, Chance, Rico and I wouldn't know what to do without you. I sometimes can't even remember what it was like not having you with us all the time. I'm grateful we have had this chance to spend time with you daily. Your Presence is a gift to all of us.

Mom (*www.RuralRouteTexas.com*), a.k.a. Dusty Rose, you were the first one who told me I could do and be anything. I believed you and here we are. I've traveled, tried new things, reached out into new worlds and found myself right back where I started–an artist, an intuitive, a writer and a curious lover of people. When I look at you, I see how your influence was there all along. From making me costumes when I was little to typing my creative writing stories in high school to crazy attention-getting trips wherever we traveled together–thanks for all you do. Thank you for being a mom that truly believed in me despite not understanding me–that's a true testimony to your heart. I know I have been unique...you were the perfect person to be my mom. You and your creative space have been a respite from the crazy world whenever I needed one most. Not everyone has a safe harbor to call mom. I love you.

Debbie Mrazek (*www.DebbieMrazek.com*), a.k.a. Memory Maker, Sanity Keeper and Seymour Group Vice President, you are the kind of friend very lucky people find in life. Like Thelma and Louise, we have blazed trails together and melted our stilettos along the way. You have held my feet to the fire to be all that I am in a way no one else has ever dared to, and I thank you for that. I thank you even more for your unconditional friendship all of these years. I love you and appreciate your huge heart.

Marta Martinez, a.k.a. The Lion Heart, you have been with me during this topsy-turvy ride that took us both into the ditch and then on the ride of our lives. Your stewpot heart gave me hope and courage during my darkest days and your little angel, Mikael, showed me the true gift of love and healing when I could barely comprehend it myself. You are a dear, dear soul sister–the sister I never had–and I am so grateful for you. I love you!

Brandie Collier (*www.ConsiderItAlreadyDone.com*), a.k.a. Chief Executive Assistant, you are truly a woman who can do it all. Thank you for helping me stay on time in this world and for loving our clients as much as we do. People tell me how much they love you, and I can see why. You have a smile in your voice for every person you meet. I trust you so very much and what a blessing you are to my heart. Thanks for always being there for me, and helping us do whatever needs to be done. The title of executive assistant doesn't really do you justice. I believe I'll just start calling you the Queen of Everything. I know it's not easy reading my mind, but you do a great job!

Holding Space Gang

I feel that thousands of angels were sent to help me embrace the ditch, plug back into my own *True You* and learn how to love myself. It has been quite the journey and I feel I have a ton of thanks to share.

Velma Gallant (*www.WelcomeChanges.com*), a.k.a. The Queen of Joy, you truly are the Queen of Joy. You were the person I trusted to help me begin healing before I could even know what the ditch was. You have become an amazing friend over the last few years and I love our friendship. It's joyful, fun and easy. The ditch has given me many gifts and you are one of the shiniest. You are a gift that keeps on giving in the form of laughter, fun and joy.

Members of the Big Blue Circle: You have opened my heart to community as family. You each have enriched the Ferguson Family life so very much in such a short time. I feel so blessed to call each of you friend, and I am grateful for every second we spend together dreaming big and reaching for the stars. Here's to going higher! Love you all so much. Together, we are quite the super power!

Members of the WISDIM Group: Each of you has filled a part of my heart. Veronica Perez Thomison (*www.MPRSource.com*) thank you for your vision that brought us together. What a gift our gatherings continue to be. To each of you who bring your special talents and gifts, I thank you for the beauty and love I receive from each one of you.

Dream Big Spiritual Mastermind Group: Minette Riordan (*www.MinetteRiordan.com*), Kathy Garland (*www.KathyGarland.com*) and Jodi Hodak (*www.WriteAwayWeb.com*). The three of you came along at just the right time for me to jump back into the land of the living. Each one of you has touched my heart in a special way and a minute lost of what we had together would have made a huge difference. I'm so grateful for our time together.

Must Be Present to Win Team

Thank you to all the reviewers for your time and care reviewing this baby: Marta Martinez, Carolyn "Nana" Badaracco, Candace Fitzpatrick (*www.CoreClarity.net*), Patty Mayeux (*www.FindELAN.com*),

Laura Armbruster (*www.ValuableConnections.com*), Debbie Mrazek (*www.The-Sales-Company.com*) and Roy Miller (*www.RGMComms.com*).

Minette Riordan, Ph.D. (*www.MinetteRiordan.com*) I have a special thank you for helping me with final edits. Thank you for 'seeing me' in these pages and helping me ensure this book is a true reflection of the work I do and who I really am. Wow, what a gift you continue to be in ways I could never have imagined when we first met at Starbucks just three years ago. I feel we have lived decades together in such a short time. You, dear soul sister, are a gift.

Jan King (*www.JanBKing.com*), Book and Publishing Consultant, thank you for an amazing book writing adventure. I had no idea at the time what a gift the actual experience of writing a book at this level would hold for me. You did, and held my hand when I wasn't sure what to do next. I will always treasure our conversations and I am so grateful for your support. Thank you for guiding and believing in me.

Tommy and Debbie Mrazek for being there when this book first came to be and for urging me to believe in it and myself. You made the trip to BEA inspirational and possible. Thank you for all the two of you have done to support my dreams and me over the years. I can't say thank you enough for your generous hearts. I love you.

Editor and Copywriting Wizard, Maria Smith (*www.TheWordsmithGroup.com*), we have worked together for more than a decade writing and editing all kinds of projects. This one, of course, was unlike the others. I so appreciate that you edit the way you do because you allow me to write the way I do with lots of emotion and exclamation points!!!! If anyone finds an error, it's only because I made a few changes AFTER you did your edits. Thank you for being you. I love your passion for words and writing.

Michelle Preast (*www.MichellePreast.com*), a.k.a. The Queen of Art-full Things & Cover Designer, you breathed new life into The Queen of Dreams artwork and have an uncanny ability to just 'know' what I'm saying when I express myself in ways that mere mortal designers wouldn't be able to begin to understand! I love your illustrations and your 'vibe'–this book would NOT be the same without your artistic ability. Thank you so much!!!

To the teachers and spiritual mentors who helped me along the way. You each continue to inspire me and I am grateful for your teachings. The world is brighter because each of you is in it: Sonia Choquette (*www.SoniaChoquette.com*), Debra Grace (*www.DebraGrace.com*), Betsy Bergstrom (*www.BetsyBergstrom.com*), Mark Stanton Welch (*www.MarkStantonWelch.com*), Steve Straus (*www.StrausUSA.com*), Vianna Stibel (*www.ThetaHealing.com*) and Hefina Glenys (*www.HefinaGlenys.com*).

Thank you to the authors who I have not yet met and who inspire me with your teachings. So many names could appear here, but two stand out for me. A special thank you to Henriette Klauser (*www.HenrietteKlauser.com*). I'm so inspired by your books. Thank you! After reading about your Seymour Group, I formed my own during my stint in the ditch, and the gifts continue to this day. I continue to look to your books as guides after more than a decade. Your ripple is huge! Violette Clark (*www.Violette.ca*) you woke up a part of me that I almost forgot existed and just in time to add an art-full flair to the worksheets that accompany this book. Your heart and spirit created a ripple effect like nothing I've ever seen. Thank you for putting *Journal Bliss* and *your* heart into print so women can embrace their inner eccentric through creativity!

To all our clients who trusted the process as we healed together and gained access to higher ground. You each have taught me so much about life. You have touched my heart so deeply. You know who you are and I am grateful our paths crossed. You contributed so much to this work and book, and I hope your journey finds you happy, whole and complete.

To all of you who listen to Queen of Dreams Radio (*www.TinaFerguson.com*) each week and have listened from the beginning, I love hearing your stories, hopes and dreams. You inspire me daily with your courage and commitment to living big. Ellen Gaines, thank you for being my number one cheerleader and also sharing your messages with me. And, to the guest hosts who share their gifts and wisdom in the world. Thank you!

Last, but certainly not least, to the Spirit World that is so rich in all things, especially love and kindness. I am so grateful for my divine connection that allows me to spend time with you. To God–the Creator of All That Is, Jesus, Mother Mary, Quan Yin, Archangel Ariel, Archangel Michael, Alliseah, Ricah, Isoah, Isla, Edena, Roger, Iragor, and the many, many other spirit messengers who uplift and support clients (and me) each and every day. I am humbled to work so intimately with you to bring healing and love to our world.

"It is by going down into the abyss that we recover the treasures of life. Where you stumble, there lies your treasure."

–Joseph Campbell

Preface

The Ditch & Dreams—A Divine Connection

Five years ago, if you would have told me the ditch is a divine invitation to begin dreaming again, I would have probably looked at you like you had totally lost your mind while pointing a finger at my temple to draw little circles in the air while mouthing, "*That's nice.*"

And, yet, here I am to tell you this very thing. The ditch you are sitting in is not a place for you to escape from, but rather a magical time out and invitation for you to dream bigger for yourself. The ditch is a cosmic time out where your heart takes you when you are woefully overdue for some time with yourself–your *True Self.*

The only issue with this whole scenario is that when you are in the ditch, you don't realize this. If only you *knew* where you are now is the *perfect* place for you.

This is why I wrote this book.

A few years ago, I fell down into the ditch and I couldn't get up. I tried to get out of it, but as hard as I tried, I just couldn't seem to pull myself 'together.' I was scared, paralyzed and I felt so alone. The more I tried to get myself out, the deeper I dug myself down into that darn ditch! If you've seen cartoons where the character is running but digging deeper into the ground with dirt flying behind making a big pile, you have a great illustration of what I was doing. I kept thinking I could get out of it, and reassured myself that I was smart enough, able enough, and doggone it; I was going to get myself out of the ditch!

But, as it turns out, that didn't happen–at least not at first, and certainly not by force.

I had never fallen down in the ditch as deeply before. I had visited for a day here or there, but never had I spent *months* there. I didn't realize it then, but the ditch was *exactly* what I needed to shake up my life, wake me up to my *True You* and invite me to start living again in *true connection* with God, The Creator of All That Is. And, wow, has my life been an adventure ever since!

When I think about why I would be writing a book about living in the present and reconnecting to dreams, the *True You* and passion, I can see why I would gravitate toward this. My life is a reflection of all of these.

I remember when I was about 16 asking my mother *what* she could have been thinking having a child in the late 60s. Conceived in late 1967, I was born on July 16, 1968. That year, the U.S. battled on both foreign and domestic soil. The Vietnam War, the Civil Rights Movement, the Feminist Movement–all were alive and well the year I came to be.

My mother was only 19. She would turn 20 six weeks after I was born. When I asked her about the chaos, the turmoil that I entered into as a baby she simply responded, "That's how life is. Some days it's good and some days it isn't. But, you don't stop living just because it isn't."

My mother who is an amazingly creative soul has a beautiful way of living in her world of art and creative spirit. I suppose I followed in her footsteps, as we are both highly intuitive and also very creative. We are creators first and foremost, and it is this artist spirit that allows us to dream from a place where those who don't venture into creative waters could never begin to understand. I believe everyone is an artist. I believe everyone has access to this dreamland. I believe everyone is a creator.

These two examples show how I view the world. One eye on the magic, the beauty, the amazing art of life, and the other on the practical, realistic understanding that life *is* life and it's up to us to make the most of it.

I believe dreams are the fuel of our soul. Dreams propel us toward what is possible even when sometimes all we can see is what isn't.

Before I was born, Martin Luther King, Jr. dreamed of a country united in race. Tragically, he died April 4, 1968. After riots broke out, the U.S. President, Lyndon B. Johnson, signed the second Civil Rights Act on April 11–just one week later–further expanding the landmark legislation from four years earlier. When John F. Kennedy talked about putting a man on the moon by the end of the 60s it was thought to be impossible. Yet, with his vision–and a nation's *dream*–ordinary men and woman followed his lead and figured out how to accomplish the extraordinary. Our first manned space flight took off the day I turned one, less than 300 miles from where I lived, and landed on the moon July 20, 1969.

Dreams do matter. The dreamer matters too. *You* are the dreamer.

I'm not sure if I am so indelibly connected to dreams because I was born in a time when dreams inspired us to reach into greater possibility, or if it was a result of my near collision with fate.

A near death experience when I was just seven months old allowed me to choose whether I wanted to continue this life. Almost unbelievably, I remember the entire sequence of events the day that I almost died of chicken pox. My fever shot to well over 105 degrees, and I was all but gone. I remember seeing my mother and grandmother arguing about what to do–I saw myself from outside of myself, and I wasn't sure if I wanted to continue on in this life. A few days later I seemed to miraculously heal overnight.

I have been dreaming for as long as I can remember. Raised with one of the earliest feminists–my grandmother; daily, I experienced a female force of nature. She was pragmatic, down to earth, saucy and hard as nails *except when it came to me.* I always wondered where she got that defiant nature and *how on Earth she lived so fearlessly.*

Born in the depression, she earned a very good living as an LVN–the type of nursing license you get when you only have a two-year degree versus a four-year degree (RN or registered nurse). She began working as a child in the late twenties picking cotton on her family's farm when she was only six, and never stopped working until Alzheimer's claimed her mind in her late 70s. Despite my grandmother's double-shifts at the nursing home where I would go with her when I was little, we seemed to always live in government-subsidized housing projects. My mother, throughout my childhood and teens, would return to these in between husbands so I clearly remember what government housing is like. I also remember the feeling of living in these places–*limited.*

For as far as I can go back into my mind I have wondered why people end up where they do in life. At five, I declared to my mother that there was a reason why some people had more than others. I seemed to 'know' that we all can achieve whatever it is we want. When I was told things were not possible when I was a little girl, I would just pray about whatever it is I wanted–asking for it, and over and over again I would be gifted with what I most desired.

Dreaming to me was, and is, like breathing. Without it, life would not be worth living.

And perhaps I believe in the power of dreams because when I was three, I had an extraordinary experience. One night, while I lay in my bed deathly afraid of the sensations I could feel of 'spirits' swirling above me, an illuminated doorway next to the actual bedroom door appeared. Through the crack in this door, a light shined so brightly that it almost seemed unreal. As fearful as I was just a few minutes before, I didn't scream because the most incredible love and peace enveloped my body. I felt safe–just like I always did when I was with my fearless grandmother. Her energy felt like a lead apron when I would sleep next to her. Only, on this night, I was staying at my mother's apartment.

A figure that looked like a man in a sparkling robe came through the door first. Around the outline of his body, I could see the most brilliant light shining. I could barely make out his face because the light around him was so bright against the darkness.

That night had started just like every other night when I was little. I had a ritual where I would lay in bed and close one eye and then the next. With one eye closed, I would pretend I was as tiny as an ant. I would imagine that if anything tried to 'get me' I could simply hide underneath the mattress, or maybe in between the mattresses. Then I would open that eye and close the other one, and would imagine I was larger than the room. If anything dared to come get me, I would simply transform into this *Alice in Wonderland* larger than myself version and I would instantly be safe because of my size.

I never stopped to consider *why* I was always so afraid. I never thought to ask anyone, either.

On this night, as this man stood in front of me, I didn't feel like running away. I suddenly felt so safe and so loved–just like I did with my grandmother. "Do not be afraid, I come to you in love," he said softly. "I will always care for you. You will always be provided for." That is what I remember most–those few messages–and the tremendous love that filled my heart and soul.

Just behind him was the most luminous angel that literally looked like a glass light-filled doll. I don't recall wings, but have always thought this woman was an angel. Her face was pure light. The two of them together were dazzling.

I don't recall hearing the exact word "Jesus," however, when I woke up that was the word that came to my little mind, and I began asking my mom to go see Jesus. I can't imagine what my mother thought when her little girl started asking to go to church. My mom was a very young mother of two by this time–and from her account I was not your typical child–often acting like a "little old lady" she has remarked. I was *quite a handful* from the stories I hear, and she allowed me to catch a bus each Sunday to go to church with the other neighborhood kids.

I only remember one thing from going to church back then. I kept asking to talk *to* Jesus, and being told that talking to Him directly wasn't possible. I wanted to *see* Him again. I kept insisting I *knew* Him, basically demanding in my headstrong way for these people to show me where He *lived.* I was told it was impossible. I was also told the bible is very clear about people who *say* they can speak to spirits. That would begin a lifelong fear of going to hell sharply contrasted against my deep desire to feel, see and talk to this loving, sparkly man who came to visit me that night. For a very long time I was deathly afraid there was something very wrong with me.

My sensitivity to the other side has always been strong. For the longest time I was terrified of the dark despite the beautiful message I had been given not to be afraid. I could feel these unseen beings and I didn't know what to do about them. They were as real to me as anything in this world. Like so many other sensitives I went through the usual process of trying to 'numb' the feelings, run away from the feelings and basically disown this part of who I am. Some of these spirits scared me, some of them felt friendly and when too many of them came around me, I felt like I was suffocating. No wonder I was afraid!

However, as I learned, and now also share with others, you can never outrun yourself.

What I didn't know during this time was that I share this gift with my family. My mother and brother are also sensitives. We all have seen ghosts in homes where we lived together while I was growing up. Many years later, we would talk about the "Colonel" who lived in our home just outside of Ft. Worth, Texas built near the area of a historic battle. Who knew that so much relief could be gained from simply talking about your experiences and learning that there is absolutely nothing wrong with you? We didn't have these conversations until I was in my mid 30s. All those years, the three of us wondered if we were imagining things and the answer was under our noses the entire time!

Throughout my childhood and teen years, no matter how fearful I would be in the dark with the Messengers, I could somehow find my way to that peaceful, loving feeling in my heart that Jesus and my guardian angel brought that night when I was three.

From the time I was 17 when I left the church I grew up in until well into my first marriage, I had been searching for an *answer* as to what to do with myself. I *knew* I wasn't evil, but what was this sensitivity and knowing that no one else seemed to be talking about or dealing with? Churches I had attended pointed to the bible to tell me that I was not 'right,' that I needed to be different. But, something in me *knew* I was exactly as God designed me to be. At three, I certainly had no idea of making any of this up, and I had literally had no religious influence to even know who Jesus was!

After I married my first husband, though, I felt like I couldn't feel my connection to God, Jesus or anything else anymore. This was my first extended stint in the ditch that I can recall. I just didn't know it then. It was a confusing time, and all I knew was I wanted more than anything to feel that loving connection again. My dreams were dried up with the lack of abundance in our life. I remember he and I drove one night over to the 'nice' neighborhood and I would say aloud, "I'm going to live in a house just like that one day." My entire life, I've always pulled myself up by my bootstraps with a new dream. If I felt down, I would just dream a new dream and get moving with God and the Messengers. That night, as I proclaimed my new dream, I had no idea how that would happen, but dreaming was just part of my make-up. I remember that not once did he ever say it too. He would always say, "Oh yeah? We'll see." Today I do live in a house similar to those I dreamed about nearly 20 years ago.

One night when I was 23, I lay awake in bed as my then husband slept. Something was not right. I didn't feel like myself. I felt unhappy and dissatisfied. My dreams were sparse. I had attended many different types of churches looking for answers. I had started studying different religions trying to figure out where I belonged. The God I had known intimately was amazing, friendly and kind. Where were the people who had seen Jesus and talked to Him? Over the years, I began to believe that it was not safe to be 'different.' That night, I prayed and asked God to please come back to me, to show me that I was loved. I had reason to believe I wouldn't be. I had done things I was not proud of over a year and a half where I was very destructive following a feeling that I didn't belong *anywhere* in this world. I wanted to forget this sensitivity that wouldn't turn off. I drank. I did drugs. I really didn't care about anything other than tuning out from myself. Of course, that was *not the way to find an answer.*

That night laying in bed, I did fear that perhaps something *was* wrong with me. But as I asked over and over again, "Please come back to me, please come back to me." I saw the most brilliant blue light come through the bedroom wall and hover over my body and then I felt this energy move through my entire body. The force was so strong that it startled me, and I didn't know what to think, but I do remember how I felt–*safe and loved.* The same, safe feeling returned again. After that, I easily found a church that acknowledged my spiritual gifts and my conscious intuitive adventure began.

First, I began serving as angels woke me up to write and deliver messages to my brother-in-law. At the time I was so grateful for the union of Spirit again that I didn't even question this. I think about it now, and wonder why. But, dutifully, I would write down pages and pages of what I was told and mail the letters. Over the years I probably sent five or six long letters to my brother-in-law who appeared to be an alcoholic musician with more lives than a cat.

During the nine years I knew him and a few prior to that, he amassed 14 DWIs, a couple of severe car accidents, one of which we came across on our way home from dinner one night. As we drove toward the flashing lights, I instantly knew he was in the wreckage. I didn't understand the connection I had to this man because we didn't really know each other that well. I continued with serving as asked. I remember the feeling of being *useful.* I believe I wanted to make up for all of my 'mistakes.'

The final letter was sent the week before he died in a Texas prison. I don't recall the specifics of the letters except that they encouraged him to be himself, and to take care of himself because he had much to share with others. After his death, we learned from other ex-inmates that he made a significant difference in the lives of many men who seemingly had 'nothing' to live for. He influenced these men tremendously and many changed their lives dramatically after meeting him. He would preach about God's love and this message transformed many of the men he met along the way.

You just never know who will be a Messenger, where a message will be delivered, or how far out the ripple will travel. *We are all Messengers for each other. Yes, that means you, too.*

I have not always acted like I cherished my gifts. I have not always acted as if I was truly protected and safe. When I look back at my life I wonder why *I* would be chosen to share with the world these messages. I have not been courageous. I have not trusted with strong, unwavering faith like many others I know. I am just an imperfect human being who has learned a lot of things the very hard way because she has not always trusted or listened.

Through all of my experiences, though, I *have* had a sense that I was being watched over. The reassurance that Jesus shared that things *would be okay.* That He would always provide for me. Whether it was only $1 left in the bank or it was an Earth Angel that showed up in my life just in time for things to work out, I *have* felt supported and protected. Most of the time, when I felt lost, I would find myself gathering tools to help others and myself, and a wonderful Earth Angel would show up and put me back onto the path.

Dreams do come true. I'm also now married to a visionary dreamer who can dream big dreams with me. By the time I reached 36, I would learn that dreaming is more about connecting with the soul than it is about accumulating material possessions. However, if we can unite race–elect an African-American president only 40 years later, and take civilians to space, then I believe we can also have some of the material things that make life sweet, too.

I have used my intuition or divine connection in every job I have held and every business I created, but I never considered this natural ability a calling. When I work with clients, I implicitly trust the Messengers and deliver the messages as they come to me. It's so easy to love other people. These unseen Messengers have been deceased relatives, angels, teachers, loving beings and religious icons. Over the years I have risen early in the morning to write letters to people to share with them a message of hope and love. I would mail these letters not knowing what the message meant or even if it would be accepted. I only hoped that I was doing what God wanted me to do.

After my son was born nearly 10 years ago, I experienced many changes that expanded my abilities rapidly and soon my intuition took center stage. I couldn't numb myself and tune it out anymore. It was 'on' 24/7 and I wanted more than anything to turn it *off.* I had no idea that this ability would save my life just a few years later. I had a *lot* of learning to do in a very short period of time. I truly had no idea how dramatically my life would change in the next decade.

Just as I had done before, I would share messages with those who were asking for answers from God. Over the course of a year and a half, many people would appear on my doorstep asking for help. Business colleagues would send people who were lost and seeking direction. It was the oddest thing. I was known as a marketing consultant, but people showed up for so much more.

For a very long time I've had an agreement with God to help whomever 'shows up'; I figured that's how I can serve and I've always been provided for. During this time, I kept saying yes even though I had no idea what to do, or why these people were showing up. I just listened and did what I was guided to do. One by one many people's lives changed. Many of these people were suicidal, many of them were depressed–all were disconnected from themselves–their essential nature. They were all *in the ditch.*

I didn't realize it at the time, but I was too. I had drifted slowly away from myself and so, unlike when I was 23, I didn't even *realize* I was in the ditch. I had many opportunities to learn from these people and also from other experiences, but I couldn't see the opportunity. It took a huge crisis and a trip deeper into the ditch to 'wake me up.'

After my own crisis, I soon learned exactly how these disconnected people *really* felt. For so long, aided by the comfort of Jesus's promise, I was a can-do person who would go after what I wanted and thrived on trying new things. I always loved to help, but I don't know that I was always compassionate. By sharp contrast, in the ditch, I found myself in a situation where I felt helpless and lost. I gained intense compassion for the suffering of others during those years, and let go of my self-righteous tendencies. I can *never* know how another person feels completely. I can only share what they feel. I also had not known what it was like to feel I was spinning in my head. I learned a great deal from my experience about what works and what doesn't with the ego and mind.

One of the most significant realizations I learned is that I didn't realize that I truly did believe that *I* was the one out in the world 'making' my dreams come true. Oh, of course, with just a *little* help from God. My disconnection brought all kinds of false stories. This crisis taught me how truly fragile and fearful I felt inside my ego. Day after day I would rise and try to sort out my confusing feelings. I felt like I couldn't get my normally peaceful mind to stop racing. I started to think in extremely limited ways–all or nothing, now or never. I wanted to be *anywhere* except where I was at the time. I wanted to escape my feelings and the present moment where I could feel every one of them. I wanted an escape button. I would imagine myself in an airplane crashing toward the ground and I desperately wanted a button that would eject me out of the plane before it became wreckage. I felt like not only could I not find the eject button, but that the plane was already in flames all around me. I began to think that my family would be better off without me. I searched for anything to bring 'me' back.

With my mind constantly racing, I couldn't hear the Messengers. I literally felt so alone. My spirit felt shattered. I remember thinking how sad it must be for people who don't usually have these heavenly beings around because I missed them so much.

I didn't ask for help–Heavenly or Earthly–because I was embarrassed. Isn't that silly? One night I fell asleep on the couch while frantically trying to figure out 'what to do' to clean up the mess I made of a business and financial failure. I felt like I was eight years old. I had just committed a terrible wrong and I had no idea what to do to clean it up. I couldn't hear guidance, so I looked for an answer on the internet. I spent hours spinning around the web desperately seeking a solution.

The next morning a solution arrived in a very different form than what I expected. An enthusiastic voice said, "Good morning!"

I slowly looked up startled by how *loud* the voice was. Drool glued my cheek to the couch. I pried the two apart and blinked a few times trying to determine if I was still dreaming. I looked around and didn't see anything.

"A duck is a duck. Why would you think you are anything other than what you are?"

By this time, I was wide awake and paying attention.

"Who are you?" I asked the unfamiliar voice.

"Who are you?" the voice asked back.

I thought to myself...*Who am I?* I don't recall an answer. I just felt the fog I had been living in, and the sharp contrast of this exuberant being sharing space with me.

That question was the beginning of my climb out of the ditch. The big ditch I lived in at the time felt like it was as big as the Grand Canyon. I felt I knew where I wanted to be, but I couldn't figure out how to get to the other side (now I know this was a sure tip-off that I was disconnected!). I had no energy and everything felt like a tremendous effort. What I couldn't know at the time is that the biggest, scariest experience of my life held the greatest gift also.

Aided by the guidance of these beautiful Messengers who answered my SOS call and many more clients who came to heal and also teach me how to return to myself, I began to put my life back together. By combining what I learned from working with other people with what I learned myself as I addressed my own return to the land of the living, the program in this book emerged.

I now know that *every* trip to the ditch holds a special gift. However, it's up to us to retrieve it while we are *there.* Plus, the trip to the ditch is *also* a gift. I wish I could have seen this at the time. I spent so much time trying to get away from it! The great news for you is that the hard work is done. These tools have assisted many people to reunite with their *True You.* I've seen clients reconnect in record time. What took me *years* to learn takes them days, weeks, months, depending on how often they show up for themselves.

Now it's your turn to take these nifty tools and put them to use in your own life and discover the gift *your* ditch has in store for you. It's time to remember the *True You.* I promise you that your gift is greater than the misery you might be feeling right now.

Until my growth from the ditch came, I had never known fearlessness like my grandmother's nature. She was *fearless.* She was a warrior. I now know my own courage and strength. And, I'm learning to fly. I'm a work in progress. I do my best each and every day. As the saying goes, *God isn't finished with me yet.*

I am grateful for the Heavenly Messengers who came to work with my clients and me, and am ever so grateful for the Earthly Messengers who brought to me their healing and teaching messages. Without my clients who had the courage to face their own crises and decide to choose life, this book (and I) would not be nearly as abundant in wisdom and story.

I believe that we are all Messengers each and every day. We are messengers of what we are. We all act as divine messengers to heal each other in all ways–always.

My prayer for you is that this book will hold you and invite you to be the light that you are. I pray it will help you answer the question...*Who am I?,* and it will show you the ditch is actually a gift you give to yourself–it's a time-out from your overworked mind. In the ditch, if you choose, you can reconnect to your heart to discuss important things like dreams, living big, and loving yourself and others.

I know, I know. . .so hard to believe, but oh so true.

Stick with me, and I'll share what I've discovered with you.

Tina Ferguson, a.k.a. The Queen of Dreams
July 2010

"Every individual has a place to fill in the world and is important in some respect whether he chooses to be so or not."

–Nathaniel Hawthorne

Introduction

Read This First: How to Get the Most Out of This Book

"I'm not sure why I can't move on things," my soon-to-be client said. "It's like I'm stuck in quick sand, and though I can see myself sinking I can't seem to motivate myself to move. I have no idea what to do with myself."

I took a sip of coffee, shifted deeper into my chair, and asked her to tell me when things started to change. "When exactly did you feel like you were starting to drift away from yourself?"

"Gee, that's a strange way to put it. But now that I think about it, I know exactly when it was."

From there, we talked for more than an hour, and by the time we finished the conversation, she had a good idea of what this 'unknown' fugue enveloping her was about, and how we would begin to work together to help her get back in touch with her Truth–her soul–her spirit.

After working with many clients over the last five years, I've noticed that the markers are often the same: ejected from life and living; looking desperately for the answers in every new therapy, trend or prescription; feeling numb and stuck; loss of interest in physical things–dressing attractively, eating well, being intimate with friends and/or a lover; robotic emotions that never seem to penetrate the overall malaise; and other symptoms that many lump into the all mighty catch-all called depression.

When I started to understand how predictable our patterns are, I realized that high functioning adults, with much less effort than they are currently exerting to 'try to get away from themselves,' could easily follow this program and gain a great deal of relief from reconnecting to their True Selves. Is this a cure-all? No. Is it possible you might be clinically depressed? Yes. Am I a doctor? No. Have I seen some of the most tragic cases shift in as little as 30 days? Absolutely.

I'm inspired to share what I have learned from clients and my personal journey so you will know, without a shadow of doubt, that you are not alone. And, even more importantly, *where you are is exactly where you are supposed to be.* The idea of being alone is the biggest trap door our minds set before us. In our misery, we believe no one understands our unique pain and suffering. How could anyone understand such despair? We create stories about how we must keep going and 'acting' like everything is okay. We deny ourselves of even the most basic courtesy to stop and rest for a while.

When you combine the idea of being alone with the false notion that you must 'get away' from where you are right now, you have a recipe for spinning out of control in your head–and in life.

I hope by seeing how common these ideas are that you will:

* Realize that you are not alone in your feelings;
* Recognize that your feelings are actually your gateway to living again;
* Know that by gently working with yourself you can return to the *True You*;
* Expect your life to improve;
* Embrace the greater possibility that is reserved especially for you;
* Begin to dream again about how sweet life can be when you are actually living it; and
* Realize that your life begins today and it begins with you.

My desire is to bring you a program that will provide a map to navigate the ditch, mine it for gold and jump back into your life. You can do this on *your own terms*. I noticed with myself and others that many of us are very successful, yet we endured treks to the ditch more often than we would like. Creating a practical, yet fun and inspiring program is how this book came to be.

A client once called me the Queen of Dreams and I love that I can be a visionary catalyst for so many to believe in the beauty of their dreams–and themselves again. The Queen of Dreams is one part grandmotherly love, one part believing spirit and one part Truth seer–just what all dreamers could use when planting the seeds of their dreams!

How to Get the Most Out of This Book

I shared my story in the Preface about reconnecting to my divine essence and God. I simply *asked*. That's all it requires. You could ask God to come back to you and begin living your essential nature *today*. By doing this, you connect to your infinite nature and *everything* in this Universe. You could ask, connect and be living life as a lottery win in as little as *five minutes from now*. This is the shortcut to the divine. You ask God to guide your life and then you follow your prompts. It's the easiest path I know of, and of course, I am telling you because I want you to live your most sacred life. When you feel and move from the love you are and the love that created you, life is simply a party of love!

If, however, your mind is busy and demands much attention (as mine did when I was in the ditch), the exercises in this book will guide you back to your divine connection. You reconnect by letting go of the things you've taken on as 'you' that are not *True You*. This book is a comprehensive toolkit created over *years* of working with clients. *Only work with the sections that resonate with you.*

This book asks you to stop often and reflect on what you believe, but when I say *you*, I don't mean the you that is your thinking, rational mind. I mean the *you* that you *know*; the part of you that yearns, the part of you that is restless, the part of you that is eager to start living again. This part of you is behind the scenes. If you are serious about getting back to the *True You* and jumping back into life, then grab a pen and work the program. Often we can confuse the idea of 'reading about doing something' with actually doing something. Our mind feels like it has done something when we buy a book, but that one action is just the first step. If we feel uncomfortable, we go buy a book so we'll 'feel better,' but once we feel better then there's no more action taken. That's akin to reading a cookbook and expecting dinner to be served!

I challenge you to put yourself *first* and to love yourself enough to peer into your amazing soul. And, don't give me any excuses about not having time to work the program because you have plenty of time already. And, by following the program, you'll have even *more* time to do what *you* want than you ever imagined. You'll be able peel away all the life substitutes that have been stealing away the lottery win called *your life.*

As you work the program, you will encounter:

- **Personal Stories:** These stories are from real people who, just like you, came back from the ditch and reunited with life.
- **Crystal Clear Clarity:** These exercises ask you to be honest with yourself, and to get clear about what you really believe about yourself, your life and your core beliefs.
- **Right Here, Right Now:** These exercises not only ask you to reflect on your Truth, they also ask you to take action.
- **True You Questions:** These are questions to answer from your Truth and to work with your soul.
- **True You Tool:** These tools are easy ways to connect to the *True You*, and include meditations, simple ways to deal with everyday challenges and other coping mechanisms that make room for you to be your most authentic self.

This book is written to meet you right where you are. It starts out in the ditch and gently guides you toward higher, lighter ground where *you* can be found. Trust yourself and go with the parts that call to you; leave the others behind. Likely, there's just one thing that can shift your entire life. Seek to *be more*, not to *do more.* Your soul already knows who you are; these tools only help you remember.

What to Expect After Reading This Book

My sincere desire is that you will feel more like 'you' when you are done working this program. When you are connected to your inner self, you will find God's love there too. This divine connection is a joyful place of knowing that makes it easier to trust everything–yourself, life, others. I know that if you work this program you will enjoy increased awareness, more joy and greater happiness about all that you are and the life you are creating each and every day.

You likely will feel safer in the world. This can lead to feelings of more trust and an ability to share more of who you are with others. Your level of expansion is up to you; how far you go is your choice. I know that wherever you are now is exactly the right place for you to dream a new dream. I also know that your desire is the catalyst for all that you are moving toward.

When I encountered my lowest days in the ditch, I would drag myself out of bed and pray for a message that would get me through the hours ahead. Often, the message would come in the form of a book title and a page number. Each message made the minutes more bearable and with each one I grew stronger. I am so grateful for the wonderful authors who have written books full of inspiring and encouraging messages. They held the flashlight for me as I fumbled around trying to find my way back to the path. I hope this book acts as a light for those who are asking to find their own light.

You are the winning ticket, yet you *must be present to win.* Not only that, but you must *play* the game of life daily to feel and know that your life, fully lived, is the lottery each and every day.

Will you awaken to all that you are and all that you can be? I hope so…the world is waiting for you–the *True You*!

Authors Note:

I have used the words
God, Spirit, Creator, All That Is,
Universe, Heavenly Messengers
interchangably throughout this book
to represent a higher power.
If you have different words for a higher power,
please infuse your own words for these.

My Promise to You

If you were working with me, you would likely be talking to me over the phone. I would listen to you fully present, aware of your energy, your breathing patterns and your essence. You would have my full attention and my true appreciation of who you are.

I would tell you it *is* possible to have the life you want. It *is* possible to get back to solid ground. It *is* possible to cut the ties that bind. It *is* possible to plug back into your passion. And, yes, you can live your life on purpose full of energy *every single day*! I would affirm that you *are* enough and that you *already* have what you need within you to create *anything* and *be* anything you desire.

I would share with you that we are about to begin a journey together and that we each must be willing to do our part. We aren't alone, so we can ask for help as we go. Heavenly support exists at every turn. Ultimately, though, it is your choice to return to the *True You*.

You will get from our work together as much as you put into it. My commitment is to bring you the tools that can assist you to maneuver any situation, to bring a structure that I know works to help people reunite with who they are and to love you unconditionally wherever you are. I know the pain you feel is not who you are. I realize you are powerful beyond measure in your Truth.

When our work is complete, you will know what takes you to the ditch and the steps to walk out of it when it appears again (and it likely will call you again, at some point, but next time you will be ready and can enter and exit by choice).

I would share with you that I do not believe in creating dependence. I'm only here to serve you. I do not need your power; do not give it to me. Use your powerful soul to uplift your life and the lives around you. You will be doing the work. Every day you will decide whether you will show up for yourself or not. Being present in your Truth is your choice. I will also share with you that these tools work amazingly fast and are easy to use. And the more you commit to using them, the faster they will deliver comfort.

Together, we would unveil the vision you have for your life–the one you've probably known for quite some time, but haven't fully believed was possible. I promise to hold and witness your vision. I will fully believe what you dream of is possible until you can do that for yourself with full faith. Will you commit to your own vision? It will be here when you are ready to hold it. The hardest step is behind you–the choice to begin is the biggest step you will take in our journey together.

I might even share what I see in your soul. I have been able to see people at this level since I was a very young child. I would paint a picture that would take your breath away. Yes, you are *that* amazing and beautiful. Perhaps I would tell you what your soul gifts are or maybe share a message from Spirit. I never know when we start what the specifics will be as I can never know exactly what the *True You* is requesting. This book is about the process that connects you to you, and connects you to all that you can see and all that you cannot see. Soon enough, if you choose, you will be connected to all of this and much, much more.

Life is a continuous ebb and flow that is like breathing. In and out. In and out. Perceived chaos never goes away, but crisis is optional.

If you will promise to use the tools, increase your self-awareness and be present as often as possible day to day, then I know your life can be dramatically different for you in just a few weeks. Many others have done it. You can, too. Our approach will be action-oriented, and will focus on stilling your mind so you can connect to all that you are. This program is not about busy-ness; it is about getting back to the business of living.

We are spiritual beings who have a life on a planet we don't fully understand–we only fool ourselves into thinking we do. This book can help you make sense of yourself. It can lead you to love yourself, too. Perhaps it will also show you how to love others who share your world.

I would urge you to give thanks in *all* things. I promise you, it's *all* good. By the time you have reconnected to the True You, you will believe that yourself.

I commit to ____ (your name goes here).

Love,

Tina Ferguson,
a.k.a. The Queen of Dreams &
Your #1 Dream Believer

Contents

Section I

Getting Out of the Ditch, a.k.a. Help, I've Fallen In and I Can't Get Out!

"Contrary to what you may think and despite appearances that may indicate otherwise, you are now in the perfect place."

–Tina Ferguson

Chapter 1
Create a Safe Place to Live The Life You Were Meant to Live

"The ache for home lives in all of us, the safe place where we can go as we are and not be questioned."

-Maya Angelou

I once worked with a 30-something woman named Tricia who was very concerned about her father. He was a diabetic, chain-smoking, overweight cynic (in her words) who was drinking himself to death. Her manner was decisive and controlled. She kept her emotions bottled up.

Underneath the surface, her own life was as chaotic as her father's was, even though the signs were absent to those around her, giving her life the illusion of order.

"I just don't know what to do with him anymore!" she vented. "I can't just let him die, but what can I do? What am I supposed to do with him?"

I asked her how his life resembled the one she was living. "Oooh, gross, you have got to be kidding. I'm not like him. I used to be overweight, but now I'm not, and I am not like him at all."

"You know, when people kill themselves slowly by overdrinking, overeating or by any other addictions, people are incensed at how that person can be so callous. 'How dare he?' 'What is she thinking?' are the judgmental comments people spew out," I said. "Have you considered that when we don't live our lives, we are doing exactly what your father is doing? The only difference is that we are doing it in the closet, without scrutiny, holed up in our little world, moving toward death faster than we are moving toward living."

As Tricia gathered her thoughts, I reflected on how deep resentments or secret envy can affect the body. This type of energy–*bitterness*–settles into the body patiently waiting for the person to deal with the remnants left over from life's traumas. I could see black energy swirling behind her as she talked about her father and I knew the repulsion she held for him was the same repulsion she held for herself.

Her silence revealed a great deal. "Your father, like you, has a choice to choose life. We can't breathe for each other," I explained. "We can't unzip him and put his body over you so you can live for him. All you can do is choose to give yourself the love you desire for him and the love you want from him. We heal others when we heal ourselves. We give others permission to be themselves when we accept ourselves. We are all together in this love soup called life."

"You are right…I can't force him to do anything. I just feel so guilty about it," she said solemnly.

"I know it is hard," I continued. "I believe the hardest thing we will ever do is watch other people not love themselves. Or perhaps watch our own lives slip by when we aren't loving–or living–ourselves."

I suggested she pray about it and ask for God's help. When we hung up, I said a prayer for her, too, and asked God to make it right for both of them so they could flourish, learn and heal.

The next day I received a call. "You'll never believe it. Another family member is going to take care of him. I'm off the hook. I think I finally get what it means to live *my* life. I know I won't be 100 percent every day, but I think he taught me a lot about living on my own terms."

Tricia and many others have used the self-love laws in this chapter to begin reclaiming their lives. These can literally take years to fully adopt and master, but every moment spent in each of them is a step toward living more authentically.

Living life on your own terms requires clearing space for you to live your most authentic life. You use obsessions and addictions to avoid dealing with what you most want to deny. You then create stories that allow you to feel comfortable in the moment and enable you to keep moving along. In this way, stories become a temporary survival tactic for perpetuating the grand illusion. With addictions and stories, there's little room for you to live. Creating a life that is true requires letting go of everything that is not true. Each time you say good-bye to something, someone or some story that holds your precious life in prison; you release space for you to live fully in a way that brings true happiness.

If you were working with me one-to-one, we would clear a space to work–not a space on a desk, but an energetic space for you to be held in until you could fully return to yourself. I would ask God to hold the space for us as we worked and I would work with you to hold your own energy. We would work together navigating the terrain of your energetic blueprint.

As you work the program in this book, I invite you to create your own safe place. This place will be your home base. The ditch may be your 'home' away from home right now and that's okay. By creating this space for yourself, you will always have these habits to rely upon should you find yourself back in this familiar territory.

These guidelines work with universal self-love laws–the Heart Flashes–that follow. They allow you to expand, breathe and fully express the *True You.* Invite your soul to come work with you as you begin and be gentle with your inner child. Welcome your Heavenly Messengers to work with you if that feels right. You may not hear them, but you will definitely feel their Presence.

We'll begin by reintroducing you to you.

Right Here, Right Now

The *True You* Meditation

Imagine something you completely and unconditionally love–a person, a pet, a sunset, a location or anything that evokes intense feelings of love. In this state of unconditional love, imagine your hand in front of you, open with your palm up. Now, in your palm, allow the image of how you see yourself now to appear. This is the self you know.

Now, begin to see the transformation of this self into the True Self–the purest essence of what you already are. This may be an animal, a light, a symbol, perhaps you as a child or even a different being from what you are in your life now.

As you see your True Self, notice how beautiful you are and how utterly amazing you are, how you are only what you experience. Notice the feeling of being in your full essence. Now, holding this True Self, see your current reality image next to it. Both are in the palm of your hand. See your current reality self merging or stepping into the True Self. In an instant, you are connected with all that you are in your infinite being.

Hold your hand in front of you and see this image as who you really are–whole, pure and completely perfect. For that is what you are. See yourself and delight in how utterly amazing you already are. When you experience the True Self, consider that you are in a state of knowing your True You.

When you experience a sense of something other than this whole, peaceful feeling, you now will immediately know that you are apart from what you truly *are* and entering what is not true–a false illusion.

If you find yourself entering into the false, just notice it. Accept it and then choose to move back to the *True You*. As you begin to experience yourself from a greater perspective, you will see yourself in new ways that show you how multifaceted you truly are.

This is who you are meant to be. No amount of struggle will ever change what you are by creation. When you use this meditation to connect to yourself, you are, in effect, connecting to All That Is and everyone else who is connected to All That Is. The connection is always there though the awareness may or may not be there, depending on your attention. There is no separation in this experience. There is simply wholeness and unity.

The by-product of the experience of self-love can't be artificially created. And this is one of the most difficult areas to master: to know one's self and to love that being completely, from the deepest part of your soul. Every part of you is lovable. With practice, you can see how truly magnificent you are. As you do, you will quite naturally find that you are also humbled by the exquisite nature of everything else you experience. That's how love grows everything.

We always want to skip what we most need to know.

If your mind is telling you, "I know this already," consider this: Are you doing it? Do you love yourself? Is your life a reflection of a person who loves the person in the mirror? Good days, bad days, bad hair days, fat days, ugly days, stress-full days: Do you love who you are?

If yucky feelings well up in your body, that's completely normal. Just put this book down and do something else. Come back to it. Take it in slowly. Work with the program; let it soak into you. Consider the Truth here and then come back for more.

This meditation is a powerful shortcut to your divine connection. If you find yourself at the other end of the spectrum in awe of yourself or weeping at the beauty of the world, this is also completely normal. Let your experience be whatever it is and know you are divine!

If you are like most of the people on the planet today, you are starving for love. You want desperately to be seen for who you *really* are. You want to release the burden of the lies you carry with you. You crave acknowledgment.

If you will allow it, this book and all the help that will come when you ask for it, will cradle you in love and will open the door to your heart. It can act as the bridge to the love you are inside your *True You*. As you read this book, and ask for the love you desire, your request will be felt and heard in your body, mind and spirit. Not only will it be heard by the parts of you, your request will be answered by those around you and those loving spirit helpers who adore you.

Crystal Clear Clarity

The People in Your Life

The people we love and who love us create one of the most sacred of safe places. Take a moment to reflect on what is true for you.

The people I feel who support me unconditionally that allow me to be me:

The people I feel who currently do not support me. Ways I can make new choices to feel better day-to-day with interactions. Some of these new choices include:

The one thing I'm craving and so hungry for right now is. I can take the following steps to give this to myself:

As you create your safe place, use the following self-love guidelines–*Heart Flashes*–to shine the light of Truth on your life and guide you to lovingly care for yourself. On the self-love road back to the *True You*, these act as road rules. Throughout the program, these will guide you to your Truth. Do your best. That's all any of us can do. If you forget, just say to yourself, "I'll do my best" that's enough to give your mind a strong direction and boost your connection to yourself.

♥ Heart Flash #1 * Stay Present

The *True You* path is littered with distractions, detours, past memories and future longings: none of these stops is as critical as staying in the here and now. This moment is the only one that affords you the opportunity to create the future you desire, to make peace with the past and to make decisions that reflect who you truly are.

You may want to think about the future, but this moment is the only place where you can actually create the future. From your thought in this moment to the action you take, the here and now is all you have.

Of all of the Heart Flashes, this is the most powerful. The present is where all power is expressed. It is the point of creation. Everything else is a Kodak moment–either picture past or picture future. Only this moment gives you the power to express your most fully-realized Self.

When you are present, your mind is not bobbing back and forth between old conversations and future appointments. You are firmly in who you are and ready to live life. Your Presence holds the infinite power you are and affords you access to insights and connectivity to everything that ever was. If that sounds like a tall order, just know that this moment is truly the gift you give to yourself.

To find your place in the present, simply tune into your body. Do this by bringing your attention to your body, notice the bottoms of your feet and the top of your head. Feel the edges of your body and bring all your thoughts back into 'you.' Take a moment and focus on your breathing and soon you will feel a *presence*–**that's you**!

Once you have connected with the *True You* a few times, a couple of breaths and an intention to be present will put you right back into your Presence.

♥ Heart Flash #2 * You Are the End of the Road

You are responsible for all you do. You are ultimately responsible for every thought, every action, every drama, every deed, every accomplishment, and every trip to the ditch you have created. No one "made" you get angry; you chose to be angry. No one made you show up late five times in a row; you chose not to find a way to show up on time. The journey to find the *True You* begins with taking total responsibility for *you.*

It also means releasing responsibility for everyone else *except* you. In the case of raising children, you are, of course, responsible for guiding them toward adulthood and independence. However, even in the case of your children, you are not responsible for their actions. They also get to choose how they act. You can guide, but as soon as you take on the emotions of their actions or what people think of them, then you are drifting over into taking responsibility for something that isn't yours.

You are responsible only for yourself. This does not mean that we can't care for others; it means we have more to care for others with. It does not mean we can't assist others, it means that we have a stronger place to assist others from when we are asked. When we focus on taking care of everyone else, it's a great excuse not to tend to our own happiness. Like Tricia in the example above, this is an easy trap to fall into–especially for those who love to serve others. "I can't because I must take care of ____________." "I would, but I can't because ______________."

The truth is that when we make other people our responsibility, we actually disempower them *and* ourselves at the same time. We say to them…"You poor thing. You are so helpless, let me help you." The catch is that when we say it to others, we also say it to ourselves. When we tell others they are powerful, we say to ourselves…"I can do it, too."

Even when it comes to caring for elderly parents and children, you can choose how you create your assistance–don't let go of your power by believing you don't have a choice. Step back from the situation and ask yourself what would be a win-win-win for everyone involved?

If you are like many of my clients, most of your challenges fall into two primary categories:

* Not taking responsibility for your own experiences
* Focusing on other people's experiences as if they are your own

If you were gasping for air because your oxygen tank is low, would you give your air mask to someone else to help him or her breathe? Of course not. Yet, that's what you do when you give the little bit of self-love you have to someone else. When we seek love from others to fill up our hearts, it's like an artificial jump-start…Splenda® for the heart.

People can give to feel better themselves. The more I love you by serving you, the more you will love me and I'll see myself in the reflection of your heart. When people give from a strong healthy foundation, there's no 'need' required from the giving. Giving and receiving are tied together. When we give because what we really want is love, then we seek external reassurance from those we serve. This can be a never-ending cycle of continually seeking outside reassurance.

When you are responsible for loving yourself, you will be able to serve and give from a full cup that never runs out. Love yourself first and love others as you love yourself.

It may seem like a paradox, but when we live from the true heart we can love ourselves, support others and have love to *spare*. We aren't trying to pour a teaspoon of love from our almost empty cup; we give from a cup that runneth over.

♥ Heart Flash #3 * Commit to Doing Your Best

Your best. Do you know what that is? What is *your* best? When was the last time you did your best? If you've spent more than a few days in the ditch, standards can slip and slide down into an unrecognizable rut.

Commit to yourself to do your best in this program and in your life. You *do* know what your best is. You know when you are operating at 90 percent of what you can do. Or 60 percent. Or even 10 percent. Once you know what your very best is you can relax. Your best is *variable.* Your best may look like 110 percent of what you know you are capable of doing at one time and only 50 percent at another time. Why? Because your best is influenced by many factors.

If you are a morning person and you work *best* in the morning, then you will be at optimal output in the morning. When you hit 5:00 p.m., your *very best* may be only 70 percent. The point is that it is your best *in this moment*. The reminder is that this moment only asks for what is *available*. So, trust that the only reason you are in that moment at that level is because *you were meant to be. Accept it.*

When you commit to do your best, you are willing to do all you can at any given moment. You are willing to live fully in that moment to the best of your ability. We feel most alive when we show up fully committed. When you understand what your best is and what it is not, then you can make deliberate choices. For example, if you don't do your best when you are emotional (and *very* few of us do), you can choose to save a conversation with a loved one until a time when you are at your best.

We can choose to be our best by choosing love and compassion–for ourselves and others, and recognize when we aren't in this place it is because we are outside of our Truth. There's no need to judge yourself harshly, just simply acknowledge an opportunity to be true to you and return to that. This is a marathon called life, not a never-ending sprint called perfection.

Heart Flash #4 * Love Yourself as Much as You Are Willing to Love Others

This is an important principle to live by. Let's say that you take responsibility (Heart Flash #2) and you do your best (Heart Flash #3) and then something happens that you don't like. It *will* happen. It *already* happens. The difference here is that when it happens *this* time, you are going to love yourself anyway and give yourself the benefit of the doubt just like you would anyone else. You will know that your life doesn't reflect one moment in time. You will forgive yourself and you will move on–quickly.

True You Tool

Connect to Love

I want you to think of something you love deeply. Is it your pet? Is it your spouse? Is it your child? Perhaps it is a place you love to visit. Maybe it's something material such as a car. It doesn't matter what you choose. Now I want you to think of this and notice the feelings in your body. Can you feel this love, this feeling throughout your body?

This is the feeling to reach for when you don't feel good about yourself. Loving yourself is more about feeling love than it is about thinking you love yourself. When you feel love, you love yourself and every cell in your body knows it. When you feel bad about something, what you are really wanting is to feel is that you are loved. And you are. This is the fastest way to remember that no matter what.

When we are kids, we learn that doing something 'wrong' is bad. Our minds put a marker down and then every time we revisit 'I've done something wrong,' our mind floods our body with chemicals that say, "Uh oh." You can easily counteract this by using this tool and connecting to love and affirming, "I'm doing my best." Step-by-step you'll get there.

♥ Heart Flash #5 * Work With What You've Got (For Now)

Part of the key to living a juicy, full life is to focus on what you have versus focusing on what you don't have. I bet your mind already knows this, but the proof is in the pudding (your thoughts being the pudding). Notice what your thoughts focus on. Is your glass half-full or half-empty?

Comparison is like poison to the mind, body and soul. The grass is always greener syndrome is a close cousin to comparison. Both lead you to a dead end.

You are an amazing person. You have so much to offer. You have so much to share. If you have been focusing on what you lack for some time, it is important for you to own what you have. What makes you uniquely 'you?' Do you tell jokes that make people laugh? Are you a good listener? Do you have an uncanny way of knowing what people need to hear?

Make a list of every single thing that you have learned, experienced and know for sure. When you are finished, take a look at all you've done so far. Get in the mood by singing a song or dancing a jig, and express all you have. No matter how silly it is (and, yes, tying your shoes counts) put it down and express it.

I haven't met one person yet who is not multitalented. So are you!

♥ Heart Flash #6 * Keep an Open Mind and Heart in All New Endeavors

Loving yourself deeply, unconditionally and fully may be a new experience for you. Keep an open mind as you follow the path. Consider that you are worth exploring and discovering all that is true about you. Realize that much of what you've been believing is true about yourself is not even true. Be willing to see the good and let go of what's false.

What if you met another person who acted as if they already knew everything about you, didn't want to hear about your dreams, ideas, and desires for the future? Furthermore, what if that person said you were stupid for wanting something more, that it wouldn't happen, that you have to be smart, thin, rich or whatever else to succeed? How long do you think you would want to know him or her? How much time would you want to spend with such a person?

Begin to think of starting a new relationship with the *True You*. Think of *you* as your new best friend. Begin treating yourself like your very own BFF (best friend forever). If you wouldn't support your best friend in a certain way, s/he wouldn't be around very long.

Keep an open mind in all you do and support yourself each step of the way. If you find yourself saying, "I know that," ask yourself, *"Yes, but am I living it?"* Integrating what you know into your experience is what turns knowledge into knowingness. Keep an open heart to all that you have to share with you. You are richly complex, wise and full of surprises. You never know what you will discover!

♥ Heart Flash #7 * Be (Gently) Honest With Yourself

The *True You* journey is between you and you. It's not between you and your parents. It's not between you and your significant other. Wow, it isn't between you and me. It's about *you*. This means that what *you* think matters. It means that the closest relationship you have is with yourself. Therefore, you must be *honest* with yourself at *all* times. When we lie to ourselves, life delivers to us others who will reflect that same dishonesty. The more courageous you can be to tell the Truth, the more you can trust everything in life. Most importantly, you can trust *yourself.*

To be gently honest means to look at an experience with an open mind and to look for the gem in it. If you snap at your lover and say something unkind, you may be gently honest with yourself and say, "That is not like me. That is the second time I've had that reaction today." If you are brutally honest with yourself, you may say, "You are so mean. Why can't you just get control of yourself?" The difference between the two is important. One is reflective, the other accusatory; one is the observer, the other the prosecutor. There's no need to pull out the judge and jury every time you step out of line with yourself. That will only serve to throw you back in the ditch over and over again to discover what is true. You have way too much living to do for that cycle.

As you are gently honest with yourself, you will find that others reflect this naturally. When you loosen the grip you have on yourself, others will, too.

♥ Heart Flash #8 * Be Kind to Yourself

What do you need? What would you like? Kindness is a way of acting out our love for ourselves and others. When we are kind to ourselves, we make our own safe place. When you have your own safe place, you won't need to look for a safe place in others. Instead, you will have room to invite others into your own safe harbor.

Just remember, though, to be kind to yourself, you must make *time* to get to know yourself. And, I don't want to hear how you can't. You can, and you will–it's your choice. Know that *you are worth it.* If I were there with you, every excuse would be taken down as fast as flapjacks–I can take down those hurdles faster than you can say "But..." Practice your own form of kindness and take down every reason why you can't and just let them go. Then get busy acting out your love for yourself.

Kindness sometimes is pushed aside in our busy world. Deadlines approach, things need to be done, yet kindness can be a way of life. Kindness is just love in action. Move yourself into love and kindness will move through you.

♥ Heart Flash #9 * Honor Your Feelings and Intuition

Feelings are those inner nudges that communicate with you. It's you and you again. This time it's your body communicating with the thinking part of you. Feelings allow the *True You* to speak to the conscious part of you. You may call this gut instinct or intuition. Feelings come in all shapes and sizes.

For purposes of this book, feelings are not emotions. A feeling with a label is called an emotion. If someone says something you don't like and you feel a lump in your throat followed by intense heat in your cheeks, you may label this feeling "embarrassment." This is important because labels ignite stored memories and past experiences. Feelings, on the other hand, can be signals–allies on your way to understanding the *True You* and what you need.

Honoring your feelings is the acknowledgment of what your True Self is communicating to you. This isn't about analyzing these feelings. It is about keeping an open line of communication between with the parts of you.

If you are dating a person and the feeling in your body is hollow and aloof, that is great information. It doesn't *mean* anything until you choose to make it mean something. When you work with your feelings, for now, all you want to do is determine if the feeling is a yes or a no. Yes feels good and feels like a magnet pulling you toward something. No feels like a repelling away from. When you feel a yes, you can make the choice to go near it or not. For a no, you can move away. Practice honoring your feelings without too much analyzing the 'data'–this will strengthen your internal connection.

This may be the hardest Heart Flash to work with because many people have learned to shut down this communication line. Feeling is a risk. It can be scary to be present and responsible for what you are feeling. However, to really live, you can't disconnect from the life you are currently residing in. The sooner you love where you are and can embrace it, the quicker you can move to a new way of living. Uncomfortable feelings are guiding you to a new choice, a new opportunity. Open up the communication line with all parts of you.

It's worth the risk, and you will soon learn that not feeling is the riskiest choice of all. Contrary to what you may believe, not feeling creates more pain than feeling ever will.

♥ Heart Flash #10 * Cut Yourself a Break and Relax

When I was about 10 years old, I was very concerned about my body not being perfect. Once, and only once, my mother told me something that changed me forever. She told me, "Relax, you aren't perfect. You are never going to be perfect, and there is always going to be someone ahead of you and someone behind you. Someone will be richer, someone poorer, someone smarter, someone dumber, someone thinner, someone fatter."

That's when it clicked that this trying to be something I wasn't didn't matter much in the grand scheme of life. Even at 10, I could feel how unhappy this fretting made me feel. I let my body worries go and accepted that I can love my body for many reasons–not just for the way it looks.

Many years later, I learned that we are all perfect in our true selves. In our eternal being, we are exactly what we are here to be. Does it mean we are perfect in our ego or personality self? No. The combination of our perfection expressing in the imperfect world we create challenges us.

So, for now, cut yourself a break. Every step forward will bring rewards you can't even imagine right now. Every courageous step you take to unfold the *True You* pays you back dividends that exponentially expand.

You were meant to live out loud, but you've got to relax the stranglehold you have on yourself to do it.

♥ Heart Flash #11 * Be Bold: You Were Born to Be!

Bold living comes from decisive living. Your decisiveness comes from clarity. Your clarity comes from the connection with the *True You*. When you commit to be bold, you are walking with yourself. You know what you believe; you understand that nothing is forever. You realize that one moment to the next, you can create again, and again, and again.

Being bold is not about pounding your chest and demanding attention like a two-year-old child. No, it is a state of being that emanates from your Truth. The more you know you, the more adventurous, assured and bold you can be.

You were born to be bold and to fully express who you are without apology. Be bold, starting today!

♥ Heart Flash #12 * Make a Commitment to Yourself

You *are* worth it. Your *life* is worth a commitment to live big. If you aren't living, then why are you here? People often ask me what the purpose is to their lives. "Why am I here?" they ask. I believe we are here to love, live our God-given lives fully and to be loved.

Your particular way of loving yourself and others is unique to you. You have dreams and desires that have been written on your heart that are yours to create with others for others.

I believe God loves us with every part of all creation. What mother or father would not want the very best for us–the fullest expression of the love we are?

When we honor our lives, our feelings, our deepest desires, we connect to our Creator who knows that we are the love we were created from. When we express ourselves from this place, we are the living Creator dancing through life. And, guess what? You can do this in your own, unique way. In fact, there's no bliss unless you find your own unique way. Yours can be a tango, a waltz or even a disco!

The day you were conceived from the seed of creation, everything that you will ever need was put into the gift that is you. The talent, the energy, the body, the understanding and the wisdom, the knowingness…the beingness…it was all rolled up into that little seed.

When you commit to yourself, you honor the creation of the being you are. Your being is worthy no matter what you have or haven't done. Because God breathed life into you, you are precious and brilliant. Do you realize how powerful you are? Do you realize that you can explore and live big? That this means that you don't *have* to do anything you don't choose to do?

As God's creation, you have the power to create. What life will you create? Will it be a quiet life of solitude? An adventure full of many people? Will you build a company? Will you write a book? Will you teach? Will you solve a world problem? What is your heart whispering to you?

The *True You* knows what you want to do. It has a way of guiding you toward it throughout your life. It knows what was wrapped in that little seed of creation. You know that you love to dance or that you love to help others. You are always speaking to you, asking yourself to come spend time with yourself.

When you bank on things outside of yourself, you miss the *True You*. You accept an imitation of the life you desire to live. When you bank on the opinions of others, the expectations of others, the traps that society feeds you, then you are living externally–relying on someone else to tell you who you are.

Define yourself! Commit to your heart's calling.

With your commitment to honor yourself and the courageous act of living your Truth, you will see an amazing life worth living that meets you every day, urging you to get out of bed and enjoy it.

Bank on yourself...you pay the highest interest.

♥ Heart Flash #13 * You Are Never, Ever Alone

A lot has been written about you and you...and, well, you. While your journey and the accompanying self-discovery really are about your heart's and soul's expansion, it doesn't mean you make this journey alone.

From the moment you breathed your very first breath, Heavenly Messengers as well as your Earthly family have accompanied you every step of the way. Along the path, you may recall Earth angels–people who showed up just in time to work with you and help lighten your load.

Of all of the messages I want to share with the world, this is the one closest to my heart. I've seen the pain that comes when people think they are 'alone.' Being alone...acting as if you are alone...all are choices. Even the most down-and-out person can find a helping hand if he or she holds out a hand to receive one.

As you make your safe place, remember that though your inner understanding is *your* journey to experience and create you'll have lots of company every step of the way.

When you need help, simply ask...here's a simple prayer I use myself and give to clients:

True You Tool

Asking Prayer

Dear God,

I have no idea what I need right now. Just send help. I trust you'll know best.

Amen.

This little tool has delivered helping hands across thousands of miles in a matter of minutes. It can work for you too. Ask. Let go. Be ready to receive.

Creating space within your mind, body and soul requires a commitment. However, it isn't necessary or even possible to master all of these immediately. Notice which ones draw your attention and start there. The answers are within you. Your heart will show you the way. Trust yourself!

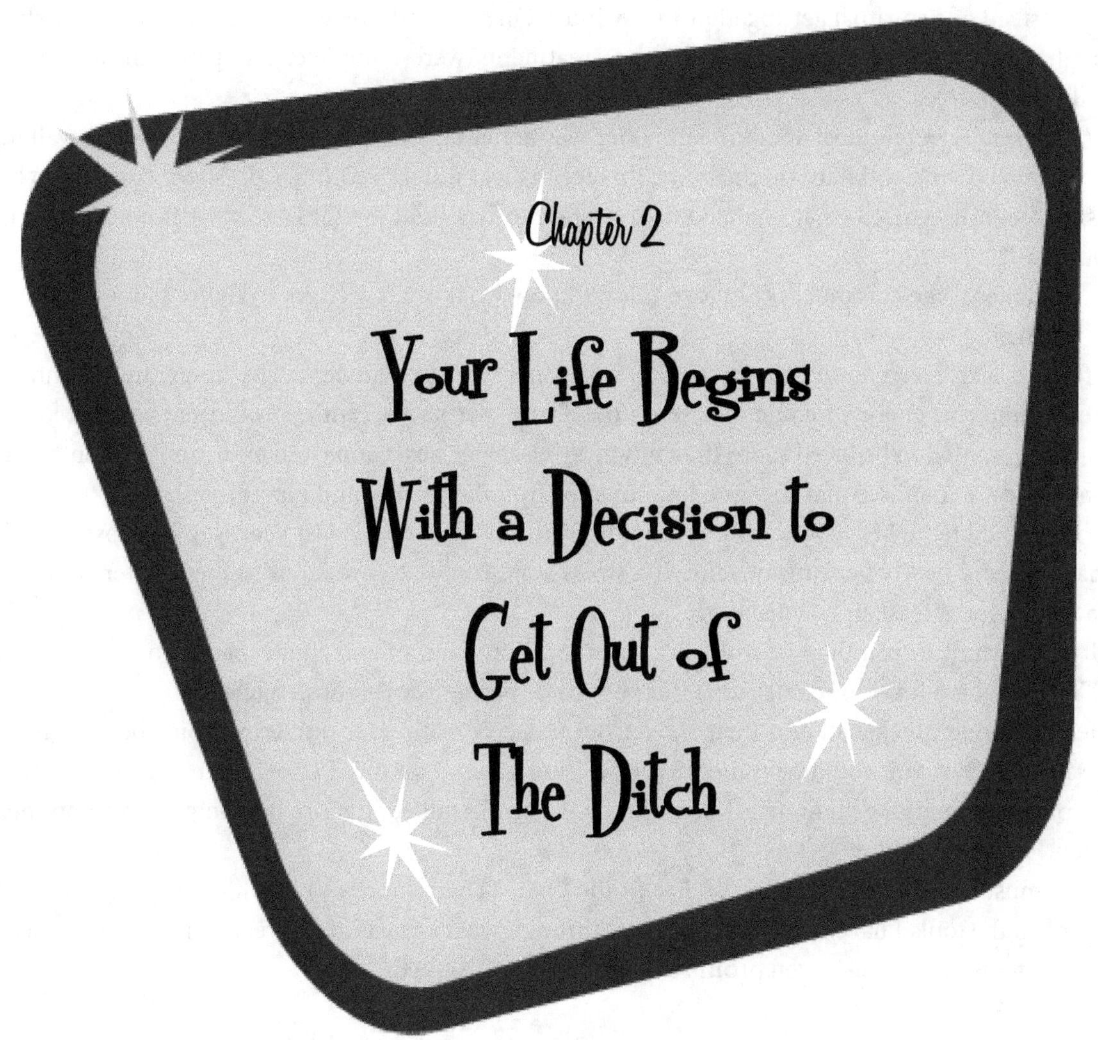

Chapter 2

Your Life Begins With a Decision to Get Out of The Ditch

"Once you make a decision, the Universe conspires to make it happen."
-Ralph Waldo Emerson

"I know you can help me," she said. "I don't know *why* I know, I just know you are the one who can help me." The woman on the phone was a person I had met only briefly once before. She was calling now because a friend had referred her to me as an intuitive mentor-coach who could help her put her life back together.

I remembered meeting the petite woman with gray-green eyes. That night, she had been stylishly dressed in white Capri pants, and a red, white and blue blouse. She looked more ready for a 4th of July bar-b-q instead of a spiritual get-together mid-winter. On her head, she wore a scarf, tied turban-style. Although I was told her breast cancer chemo treatments were complete, I did not know she was officially cancer-free.

What I remembered most about meeting her was her energy. It was hollow–empty, like a walking corpse. I knew chemo was hard on the body; this feeling was a stark reminder. In sharp contrast to her tired skin, her eyes danced when she talked. It is said the eyes hold the soul's secrets, and hers were no exception.

"I need help," she continued. "I'm lost. I don't know what to do. I've got to figure out a way to get out of this hell."

I felt her fear. Her knotted energy held her prisoner, and I could sense she desperately wanted a lifeline. Behind this energy, I could also sense the Truth–her soul's Truth. I could see her as a loving woman who wanted to be loved more than anything else. Her heart appeared enormous in contrast to her small body. I could see that she was disconnected from her loving and playful soul.

Who could blame her for wanting to unplug from this life? In the last year, she had lost her job, her marriage and nearly her precious life. If a stress scale could be compared to the Richter scale, she would be due for at least an 8.7 quake.

"I will commit to you that we will work together. You have an amazing capacity to love, Judy," I said. "Your soul is a lover, not a fighter. Life is not meant to be a constant struggle."

Her breathing quickened and then she let out a deep breath. Her quivering voice became more deliberate. "I knew you could help me. If you will not give up on me, I know I can get through this. Please, please do not give up on me. I don't know if I can handle one more person giving up on me," she cried.

"You must not give up on *yourself*," I reminded her. "There's more to this life than you can see. I will share all the tools I have. I will help you sort through what's real and not real. And, I will stay with you no matter what as long as you promise to do your part. Agreed?"

"Agreed."

Within two months, Judy moved from homeless and living in her car to having a job and a new home. These transformations stemmed from *deliberate choices* on Judy's part. She chose to look at her experience, end the helplessness and move to *conscious choice.*

I've worked with other extreme cases like Judy's where the person *chose to live.* Her situation and others may be called crisis. I call it disconnection. I call it being unplugged from you–the *True You.*

While Judy's experience may sound harsh compared to yours, it is really no different. The feelings are the same. The emotions are similar. The steps are the same. What brings one person to the brink may be a walk in the park for someone else. The point is it doesn't matter. If you are feeling disconnected, you have a choice–the choice to live or to only exist. Those who find their way to my door choose to live.

Disconnected people say, "I'm just not myself." Or "I don't know what's wrong with me." Or "I just feel so blah." Or "I can't get motivated." Many people feel disconnected. Your feelings are not unique. You are not alone with your unplugged feelings.

When a famous person such as Heath Ledger or Chris Farley dies of a drug overdose, people often comment, "I can't believe it. That person had everything to live for!"

You have everything to live for, too! When you choose to live your life connected fully to God, who you are and those around you, you can create *anything you dream of.* Your life can be every bit as amazing as you might think theirs is–without the tragic ending. Remember, *you* create the life you love to live. And, only you can create it *your way.*

Just like you, at some point, that famous person who abused drugs was disconnected. The space between the *True You* and the place where you are living is a ditch–a crack in the pieces of you. I also call it the land of nothingness because not much happens here.

When you are disconnected, you are trying to fill the gap with something–*anything*–that will enable you to feel alive again or forget the gap exists. Some fill it with drinking, drugs, TV, food, sleep, video games and shopping. These are all desensitizers–cheap replacements for what you really want–YOU! These take you *away* from your life. They move you *away* from living fully and feeling deeply. You may argue that they take you away from pain, yet living is full of feelings, including pain. I promise you that the most amazing life is worth the pain that is in it.

Your feelings create a space for you to connect with yourself and others. They sing the language of life. My clients share that they quit feeling a long time ago because it was just too painful. I believe it is not because it is too painful, but because you do not have the tools to deal with the occasional pain you experience. Your life has so much to give you. You have so much life to give!

Ditch-less Living–Take the Road Less Traveled

Imagine you are standing at a fork in the road. One of the roads is narrow and unpaved, full of small and large rocks. As you peer down this road, you can see a crooked path with corkscrew curves. The road is narrow, overcrowded with lots of aggressive people in small, boxy cars. The scene is chaotic with the drivers honking and trying to edge others out of the lead. Not far in the distance, there is a steep incline where you can see a huge traffic jam. There are no signs along the side of the road; in fact, there are no rest stops, either. There is no question this is the bumpier, harder road of the two. On this road, the people experience 'not enough' and 'just enough.' The road is exhausting and full of struggle. It feels like a treadmill because there is never time to rest.

The other road before you is paved. It's much wider. There are a few bumps along the way, but nothing that can't be easily handled by the people driving peacefully in their shiny, well-maintained cars. Signs line the road to assist you on your path. Along the way, there are plenty of people willing to lend a hand if you need it, and there are many unseen helpers guiding you to the best people who will make your journey easier. On this road, you experience 'plenty' and 'more than enough.' People on this road do their part and help others do their part. It's a road with more than enough cooperation and collaboration.

The first road is called Struggle Street. It's crowded because so many people have chosen this path. The good news is that you will always have complaining buddies to keep you company if you choose it. About 97 percent of the world's population is found here.

The reason is very simple, albeit hard to believe.

The reason is that they don't believe the second gold-lined, green lights only street–Easy Street–exists. So they never bother picking up a map to determine how to get there. Even those who believe Easy Street exists end up getting lost along the way because they keep using the rules of the road from Struggle Street. They eventually maneuver back to where they came from–Struggle Street. Good news! You already have the new road rules–they are your Heart Flashes from Chapter 1.

I want you to know that it *is* possible to find Easy Street *and thrive* there.

Right Here, Right Now

Choosing Your Life Path

Which road would you take? What thoughts come to your mind about this?

Which road are you on now? Thoughts or feelings about this?

Is it time to switch? Remember, by making a *true decision* to switch, the forces of everything in the Universe move with your heart's desire. As soon as you say, "Yes!" the whole world says, "Yes!" to you as well. Isn't that exciting? Write your thoughts here:

Two Turnpikes Take You to Easy Street

The Past Perfect Turnpike is one way to exit to Easy Street–if you want to take the long way around. It will take years–many years–to get to Easy Street using this turnpike. It requires intense determination. You actually journey back in time, take a look at everything that didn't work, filter through your feelings about your mom, your dad, your siblings, your co-workers and any other person who may have harmed you in your lifetime. Once you identify all these things, you make peace with your feelings and the people involved in creating those feelings. Be sure to remember to make peace with yourself, too. Once you do the major clean up on your past journey, then you will feel okay and can begin slowly to merge onto Easy Street.

The Fast Forward turnpike is the way to make your way to Easy Street in record time–starting today! You spend a short amount of time doctoring any fresh wounds you currently may be nursing and then focus on the trip ahead.

Most of your attention is spent in the present moment–in action–creating your future. It doesn't require that you be clear, perfect or anything else other than whom you are right now. When you bump into things that request your attention, you deal with them. The longer you spend on Easy Street, the easier it is to be clear and more of who you are. I say, "The sooner you get to Easy Street, the better!"

Both of these turnpikes will take you out of struggle. Fast Forward will take you there much faster and with a lot less effort. Make no mistake, though, you will have to do your part along the way. There are no chauffeur-driven limousines on this route, although it may feel almost as easy. In your awakened life, you are in the driver's seat behind the wheel.

When you work with Fast Forward, your movement blows away the residue and helps you learn about yourself in real time. There's not a phase before something happens. You clear away the cobwebs *while* you are living your life. Past Perfect finds the mystic on the mountaintop, and the Fast Forward finds the mystic in the city surrounded by people, life and a whole lot of living.

Choosing the Road Less Traveled

You may be wondering why anyone would choose Struggle Street when Easy Street is just as accessible. Remember, most people can't see the off ramp to jump off of Struggle Street. They have accepted that Struggle Street is reality and that there's absolutely no choice in the matter. This is because, usually, their parents live on Struggle Street; their friends live there, too. Soon enough, Struggle Street is all they know and they can't trust anything else.

Some make it over to Easy Street, but since they don't know the road rules there, they soon find themselves returning to what they do know and what feels familiar–and they're back on Struggle Street once again.

When you discover that you are responsible for yourself, and see that *every choice* is *your choice*, then you begin to see the off ramps. When you are dissatisfied and feel trapped in a dead-end job or dead-end relationship, you will know without a doubt that you are there by choice. You *always* have a choice. It may not be a perfect choice or solution, but another choice is always available. With each progressive choice, you begin to break out of your box. Your possibilities open up, and soon you are acting on them!

Benefits on the Road Less Traveled

Many benefits accompany the road less traveled. First of all, there are fewer people on it, and many of these people are more supportive and less competitive than those who dwell on Struggle Street. That means that you can reach your destination *much faster*.

Easy Street requires effort; however, you leverage that effort so you are not doing everything by yourself. On this road, you don't even believe you can do it alone so you don't even try. When you hit a roadblock, it's not the end of the world because you know it's not you, alone, against the world. Easy Street is *more collaborative.*

You will have plenty of energy on this road less traveled. When you hit bumps along the way (and you will), you won't bottom out like you would if you were on Struggle Street. The bumps in the road will feel like mere pebbles as you move swiftly over them. This road is *much easier.*

With signs at every turn, the people who greet you, the unseen helpers that support you and the joy you get from actually *living,* this is one road that carries *more fun.* Wouldn't you like to leave the struggle behind and have more fun?

The most compelling reason for making an exit to the road less traveled is because *it works.* The *True You* isn't looking outside of you for the answers. Your True Self knows that all you are dreaming of is possible and completely available to you. Everything you need to get back to you is in you. It's a cakewalk from here!

Mind Candy * Something for Your Logical Side to Chew On

The mindset of struggle is alive and well today. People stay on Struggle Street because they don't have the owner's manual for Easy Street. People don't take the road less traveled because they believe in the lie of struggle. They believe what they see. Then, they become what they believe. And, soon it starts all over again. Struggle is a habit, and for some, the drama of the struggle habit is addictive. They are literally addicted to the woe-is-me story. It has hypnotized them into a trance that is a poor substitute for living.

Life is as complex as you care to make it. Getting to Easy Street is no harder than the steps outlined in this program. You may question that. Your mind may say it *has* to be harder than that, and that is exactly what those on Struggle Street would have you believe. What do *you* believe? Do you want to try something new? How about starting *today?*

The amount of work, the energy, the resources you are exerting now are no more than you will use on Easy Street. It may feel like more work initially because you will be flexing muscles you may not have used in your entire life. Remember when you first began driving a car and it felt that it took your entire mind's attention to master driving a car down the road?

Well, just like learning to drive, with diligence, you will very soon be floating down Easy Street.

Lies Found on Struggle Street–Do You Believe Any of These?

* Few people get what they want in life.
* You have to do what you have to do, and then you get to be yourself when it's all done.
* Only ________________[insert luckier group here] get to do what they want and be what they want.
* I'm no better than anyone else; why should I want anything better?
* I can't be true to myself and be successful. I would rather be successful.

Traveling on (or choosing) Easy Street works. And, it certainly is a much more scenic route!

If you are ready to commit to living a life on Easy Street, supported by all that you are and divine support systems, and you want to make a *true decision,* then commit now with the following commitment to yourself. Remember, if you are feeling overwhelmed, just put this book down and go take a walk and practice being present by focusing on your body. You can do this!

I Commit

- I hereby commit to honor the art of living fully, completely and creatively.
- I live in the present, united with my Presence.
- I honor my needs and consider what I desire as often as I consider the needs of the people around me.
- I do my best at all times and increase my awareness of what my best is and what it is not.
- I am honest with myself. I tell myself the Truth.
- When I am learning, I am gentle with myself as I explore my new landscape. I understand I am not here to strive to be anything more than that which I am.
- I accept the support and love of those around me. In both the seen world and the unseen world, I know God surrounds me with all I need to accomplish all that I dream of and desire.
- I see myself as an extension of a Creator who knows all, and in this, I accept the gifts that come with my beingness.
- I focus on what I already have with a grateful heart, realizing that by creating this moment fully present I move quickly to those new experiences I am creating.
- I am responsible for myself. When I take full responsibility for myself, I realize I can help others even more—if and when I choose.
- I make choices because they are right for me, and when I say no, it is because I choose to say yes to myself and no to working under obligation.
- I commit to living the life I know I choose to live. I commit to my greatness. I commit to all the parts of me—all that I am.
- I commit to myself to create an art-full, beauty-full, grace-full life.
- I am worth it.
- I am ready for my new life!

Signed ______________________________

Date ______________________________

True You Question

Where are you now?

Do you remember what it feels like to feel fully alive? To feel full of life? Are you ready to do something different? If so, let's go. It's time to connect to the Truth of where you are in your life.

When was the last time you felt deeply satisfied with your life? What was happening at that time?

Go back to a moment in your life where you felt fully alive. Describe it in detail. Trust the very first thought that comes to your mind.

Name three things you love to do that make you feel truly alive (it doesn't matter if you haven't done it in 10 years or 10 months).

Name one person whose Presence feels full of life to you (you do not need to know this person well–the focus is on getting in touch with what a full life feels like). What is the feeling you identify with most within this person?

Complete this sentence. If I choose to live my life fully, ***so*** many wonderful things would happen. Some of these things are:

Keep going! Let your heart show you what you most desire.

Your life is given to you free of charge and you can create with it what you like. This is a great place to start. If you are looking for a quick, sure-fire formula to step out of the ditch, see page 199. Remember, this program is designed to enhance your relationship with your *True You*. I *know* you can do this!

Chapter 3
Moving From In The Ditch To Ditch-less Living

"Some artists shrink from self-awareness, fearing that it will destroy their unique gifts and even their desire to create. The truth of the matter is quite opposite."

-James Broughton

"I can feel it coming on," he said, swallowing hard to keep the emotion down. "Black ice is what I call it. It's as if everything is going great and then I hit the skids and everything goes into a black hole. From that point, I can't seem to get myself to do *anything*. All I can do is turn on the robot and act like an android."

Chad a tall, model-looking man seemingly had everything at his fingertips. A talented professional who helped business owners harness the power of technology, he was married to the love of his life, had two great kids and a flourishing business.

"I don't know how to get off the ice," he continued. "Maybe I'm just depressed. Yes, that's it. But I've tried all kinds of medications and nothing seems to work when I hit the ice."

"Let's take a look at what happens just before you hit the ice so we can determine what's going on and how you can be more aware of what precedes it," I said, sifting through his layers of confusion and feelings of being overwhelmed. "Your life and work are important–but it is *you* that is most important," I reassured him. "I know you can do this. Let's determine a plan to get you moving so you can grab your gift and get out of the ditch and off the ice."

Are you in the ditch? Feeling the cooling effects of black ice? People in the ditch are like the walking dead. It's like living in monochrome–a lackluster existence where life has lost its color and vibrancy. From my experience with clients, people in the ditch may notice:

* Loss of interest in activities they used to enjoy.
* A bland malaise with little variance in likes and dislikes.
* Unable to make decisions.
* Feel irritable and helpless.
* Feel they are trapped in their bodies–their minds are moving, but their bodies don't want to go anywhere.
* Feel overwhelmed or apathetic.
* Have a desire to change but are unable to take action.
* Feel they are just going through the motions.

This state of being is often labeled depression. Some people are clinically depressed and take medication for it. Yet there are many more depressed people who take medication and still feel that something is not right. They know only too well that they aren't 'themselves,' and the feelings of depression aren't completely gone, either.

Astonishingly, some people have no idea they are even depressed until they buckle one day under the burden of living in such a low place. Many people have never felt joy, and so the ditch is a familiar place to live.

I mostly work with high-functioning individuals who have drifted away from who they are. High-functioning people slide under the radar because they can force themselves through a day. They don't hit the snooze button one too many times. They can hold down a day job. They are reliable–almost to a fault. In fact, this 'will do' attitude is often what keeps them stuck even longer; muscling through everything they *must* do instead of what is *important to attend to–the True You!*

Their experience is subtle at first, like adding a few pounds here and there; it isn't noticed until the person finds him- or herself squarely in the ditch.

The ditch is a gift, but it can't be a place for you to spend time with yourself if you spend most of your time trying to forget you are there in the first place. Chapter 1 showed you how to access what you want most (you and love for yourself) and how to give that to yourself so you can move out of the ditch.

Our goal here is to help you identify and become aware of the signs that alert you that you are *headed* for the ditch so you can begin to be more self-aware and honor your mind-body-spirit connection.

Each of you is slightly different, yet there are *always* similar signs:

- Experiencing a catalyst event.
- Ignoring it, pushing it down.
- Avoiding the warning signs that the ditch is approaching.
- Entering the ditch.
- Being fully engulfed by the ditch.

Getting to Know Your Ditch

When was the last time you were in the ditch? How did you feel? What do you think you really needed (What was the gift that you received from being in the ditch)?

Describe what sends you into the ditch. What you do after the catalyst event? How long does it take you to realize you are in the ditch? What is your preferred way of dealing with or exiting the ditch? Conscious awareness is the key to managing its effects.

What sends me off into the ditch is:

After that, I usually:

It takes me ______________________ amount of time to realize I'm in the ditch.

To get out of the ditch, I usually:

Adventures in the Ditch

One client described her experience with the ditch in great detail. With some effort, she was able to address the key signs that signaled the ditch was approaching.

The first sign was a flush of feeling like she wanted to run away. She described it as a heaviness that would sweep over her that began as a feeling of being overwhelmed in her current activity. As a business owner, the endless emails, details, phone calls, tugs from clients and business details, combined with the responsibilities she felt at home, were enough to throw her in the ditch on a regular basis. She felt like she was not enough and could not handle all the demands on her attention, mind, body and, ultimately, her spirit.

When we first started working together, the frequency of going into the ditch was every three to four months, and the episode lasted about two to three weeks. If you do the math, this vibrant woman was losing about two months every year to the ditch–definitely not the way to live a full life!

After our initial consultation, we identified a theme and the preceding signs that the ditch was beckoning. Our approach in this program is to work with it. Rather than avoiding the ditch or running away from it, we make peace with the present. We honor the ditch's presence and realize that it is here to help support us in what we truly need and are asking for at a soul level.

Making peace with the ditch is more about understanding why you are moved to go there. From what I see with clients, the ditch comes when you aren't honoring who you truly are, what you truly want and what you know is possible. It arrives to remind you that you always have a *choice*–and that you are also abundantly supported. Remember, all you need to do is *ask for what you want.*

For this client, as with many clients, the ditch begins with 'too much thinking.' The overwhelm was a sign that she needed a break–physically and mentally.

This gave her an opportunity to honor what her body needed–and her soul's thirst. With this awareness, she could see her overwhelming feelings as an invitation for play, activity or rest. Instead of batting at the overwhelm like a pesky insect buzzing around her workspace, she now had language to identify what was happening to her.

"Aaah, I need a break–yes, that's what is happening." Or, "I need to have some fun; I've been working way too much."

With most of us, this kind of strategy is counterintuitive. When you feel overwhelmed, shouldn't you just keep plugging away at it so you can get the overwhelm under control? While that *sounds* like a good idea, it rarely works.

What *does* happen goes something like this:

You wake up. Whatever you have scheduled for the day doesn't sound appealing. You go through your routine to get ready–shower, brush teeth, get dressed, eat breakfast (or not, depending on how far you are moving toward the ditch). You don't really feel like doing whatever you *have* to do, but you do it. Let's say, for example, what you don't want to do is work. Okay, so you arrive at work. You are waiting for motivation or inspiration and, since it hasn't arrived, you decide to check email. The list begins to grow. You still don't feel like working so, hey, here's an article to read and there's a viral video to watch sent via email by a friend. It's already 10:00 a.m., and you haven't done anything so you feel a twinge of guilt as you go to grab another cup o' Joe so you can get through to lunch. You walk back to your office and decide, "I've really *got* to do something today!" So, you choose a very unintimidating, unimportant task that will give you a sense of accomplishment (or not). The day continues in this fashion while you keep thinking, *'I can catch up later. I can work later. I'll do it tonight when I get home. I'll do it tomorrow.'* On and on it goes until you've spent almost an entire day doing little to nothing according to what you believe is acceptable.

People who go through a Monday like this can usually kick-start themselves by Tuesday. Those who are headed to the ditch will find Tuesday running much like Monday and Wednesday following course. Day after day is the same. You check deadlines…"I can let this slide and then make up the time later." The more you fight it, the more time you burn on things you couldn't care less about. The longer it goes on, the bigger the tidal wave of overwhelm, guilt and shame. It builds to the point where you get sick, check out or just muscle through.

People relate to this cycle all too well. Yet, when asked why they don't go ahead and take a mental holiday they persist in the illusion that they don't have *time* to take one. In reality, they *are* taking time– *lots* of it –but in a way that isn't healthy or productive.

The ditch is a time out. Do you want to spend time *in the ditch* retrieving time with yourself, or would you like to proactively spend time with yourself? The choice is yours.

Eventually, a release comes and the ditch abates…but how did that happen? You won't know until you choose to face it fully conscious for yourself.

Make friends with the ditch. It's your natural way of calling the *True You* home.

Distractions are a tip-off that the ditch is near. In and of themselves distractions are not bad; in fact, they are often activities that invite us to *do something different.* When these beckon and you know something else is more pressing, pay attention. You have an opportunity to make a *choice* about how you choose to live your life.

You may distract yourself with meaningless chores such as:

* Cleaning the office.
* Cleaning the email inbox.
* Checking email (looking for input).
* Checking voicemail (looking for something that is more urgent).
* Opening mail.
* Flipping through magazines or catalogs.
* Calling people you don't *need* to call, inviting a long conversation you really don't have time to have.
* Answering the phone call from someone you know will ask for a great deal of your time.
* Turning to any one of your many addictions.

Crystal Clear Clarity

Your Favorite Distractions

No judgment, only information gathering and building self-awareness. These are the activities you use to tune out when you are bored, unsatisfied or feeling unmotivated. Note your favorite distractions:

After looking at your life, your patterns and themes, I believe you will agree that when you are in this state, you really aren't getting much done anyway. So why not honor what you need and give it to yourself? As funny as it sounds, you can save yourself hours– *even days* –by giving yourself some 'you' time.

Our world has created a society that loves to struggle and suffer. The more you suffer and struggle, the better you fit in with all the other strugglers. The media feeds on drama and controversy is king. Some people are addicted to drama too. Living a *True You* life, you find that life expands and constricts around you. God is always around you, supporting and providing what will help you to be your best.

Now, here's the secret. In our crazy, information-overloaded world, many of us feel squeezed for time. The key to understanding and using these tools is to realize that you don't always need a full day off. Perhaps you will choose to take one here and there, but more often than not, you need something specific and just a little bit of it.

The client above needed nature. Her work was all about computers and technology. There were so many details she attended to; it was easy to get overwhelmed. Her body, mind and soul beckoned her to go outside. She found a love of bicycling that propelled her forward. She also enjoyed mowing the grass. Like many of us in our technologically advanced world, her work didn't give her an immediate feeling of accomplishment–her projects would often span many months, if not years. Completing something and feeling a sense of accomplishment was really a way to *feel* good. Mowing the grass put her squarely into nature while also giving her a sense of *accomplishing* something. She could stand back and look at the lawn and know it was 'done'–this was a true contrast with her never-ending projects in her business.

She needed to return to nature and honor that her adventurer spirit loved to travel. Bicycling was a great way to plug into that part of her. At the same time, her inner workhorse needed to finish *a race*–it didn't need to finish everything, just *something.*

By understanding that sitting for hours in front of the computer (being busy and yet not really doing anything, i.e., reading email, cleaning out the inbox, cruising the internet) did not get anything accomplished and certainly did not serve her, she was able to let go of the longstanding beliefs she had about forcing herself to muscle through when her body and soul were drawing her attention toward something else.

I find that many people are afraid of letting go of the reins. They are so used to ignoring what their bodies, their hearts and their minds desire; they are afraid they'll get lazy and that they'll turn into unproductive sloths. Nothing could be farther from the Truth. In fact, most people report that by using these tools they get *more* done than they have in *years!*

What works for you will be unique to you. When you begin to actively communicate with the many parts of you and learn that *you* are so *wise*, you will begin to see how important this is and how it can dramatically change your life!

Our bodies hold on to lots of information we can't deal with at the time. God has infinitely provided so much support in each one of us that there is ample room to stuff and stuff away the things that are bothering us. When I see how adaptable our bodies are, I am in awe of how complex we are and how beautifully resilient we were designed to be.

True You Tool

Body Awareness

Here's an easy way to tune into your body to get guidance to know where to start.

1. First, take some deep breaths, deep into the belly and into the bottom part of your lungs. Notice your lower abdomen rising and lowering with this deep breath.
2. Next, notice a part of your body that is calling your attention to it. You might have an ache or a pain, or your attention may simply be pulled toward it much like when you are attracted to something you like in a store–you are drawn toward it.
3. Focus your attention on that area and then ask, "What do I need to know right now?"
4. Notice the answers that pop into your mind.
5. Record your answers here:

The answers could be something you need to give yourself, or something you have forgotten, or something you really need to be aware of–perhaps something you've been ignoring. It may also be a reminder to honor who you are–not what you've been pretending to be. God has given us wise hearts, wise minds and wise bodies. It's up to us to reach in and access that wisdom.

Steps Out of the Ditch

The steps out are similar for most people. First, you must calm your mind and release the swirling energy that is overwhelming you. One of the best ways to do this is to journal what's on your mind. By pouring out all of your entangled thoughts (and their accompanying energy) onto the page, the thoughts become more manageable. Remember, when you are in the ditch, you are disconnected from yourself so your sense of perception around the Truth is off as well. In the next chapter, I'll help you sort through your thoughts. For now, just let them out of you.

Here are a couple of ways to journal:

* **Write in a stream of consciousness, as quickly as you can without stopping.** This is what my eighth-grade English teacher, Miss Bibby, called pushing the pen. If you are stuck, just write the first thing you see around you. If you don't like what's coming out, remember that you can always burn it later. This is like sanity in a bottle, so give it a try.
* **Dump everything you are holding in your mind.** Your mind is a receiver, not a trash bin, a memo pad or purse. Write out all of your mental to-do lists. Make one for home, one for office, one for things you ought to do, one for things you want to do. No rules here, just write what feels right. If you want, you can use a free form downloadable from my site http://www.TinaFerguson.com/mbp

Nothing Happens Until Something Moves
Working with Purposeful and Inspired Action

The next step is to get into two types of action–*purposeful* and *inspired.* By being in purposeful action, you reconnect to your body. In the ditch, you are like a helium balloon with most of your energy and attention directed toward your thoughts. Thoughts swirl about, but not a lot of thinking is actually happening. Thoughts are not conscious thinking. More on this later. Also, when you are stuck in your head with a million random thoughts crowding out the *True You*, there's not much happening. The reason is simple–without a decision and a clear focus, nothing moves. With purposeful action, you can reconnect to the *True You*–and to your body.

Purposeful action is movement with deliberate intention. The more rhythmic and repetitive, the better it will work for you. The goal is to be in your body, in the present–not just going through the motions.

The basis of this program is reconnecting to *you.* And, *you,* can only be found in this moment. This means that if you go for a walk, you don't take an audio book so you can check out again. When you show up fully present and available to what *is* in this moment, you might take in the feeling of your feet on the pavement, or you may notice the shades of pink on a single rose, it means that you feel alive–fully present and awake.

Some purposeful actions you may want to enjoy:

* Walking
* Jogging or running
* Cycling
* Tai chi or other martial arts
* Swimming
* Yoga
* Household activities such as vacuuming, scrubbing the tub, washing dishes, folding clothes
* Crafts such as refinishing furniture, painting, sanding, knitting, needlepoint

Once you have released the mental emergency valve and have reconnected to your body, it's much, much easier to be aware of what you are experiencing and what you want. With this heightened awareness, try giving yourself whatever it is you are most hungry for and notice what happens.

When you are present and courageous enough to face your 'now,' you will experience moments of grace and gratitude that will take your breath away. This happens when you are connected to you and to everything else, including God. When you have a flash of inspiration, trust these and you will find yourself naturally taking inspired action.

What is the ditch allowing you to avoid?

No matter how long you've been in the ditch, likely you are there because you are trying to avoid something in the present. What is it? Be truthful. If you honestly don't know, just ask yourself, '*What am I avoiding in the present?*' Then go take a walk and see what comes to mind. The answer *will* come. However, you must have the courage to ask the question first.

For example, with money issues, there are only two ways to move–toward a solution or toward more of the challenge at hand. Avoiding the overdue notices piled on the floor takes you toward the challenge while the truth is, a solution is just around the corner. Take a moment and face your fears. What else is requesting your attention?

As your Queen of Dreams, I promise only to bring you tools and experiences that will take you to a lighter, brighter life. While this may look daunting, the truth is that if you will take action on the things you are avoiding, you'll feel much, much better in no time flat. You do not need to know the answer to get started–this is a trap door your mind has for you. All you need to know is what you want next and/or how you want to *feel.* As with the example above, if money is a worry, then you may want to feel *secure* or you may want to feel *rich* or *abundant.* Simply ask to connect to a time when you felt this, and instantly you will be connected to Truth in that moment. It really is this easy to shift how you *feel,* and therefore what you create!

I once worked with a woman who was in the middle of trying to run away from everything in her life. Christy grew up doing for everyone else, and so by the time she hit 34, she was buried in family responsibilities that simply were not hers to own. She didn't even realize that she was not attending to her own needs until she landed in the ditch, paralyzed by the fear of life itself. This paralysis brought her to a point where she was forced to learn how to ask for help. We worked together to identify the actions she already knew she needed to take, but was not taking.

Her list looked something like this:

- ***Follow up on overdue client invoices.** Lack of follow up was the reason for her lack of business income; however, because she believed she was terrible at managing money, she avoided the subject all together.*
- ***Hire a bookkeeper.** Despite the idea that she did not have enough money to hire a bookkeeper, getting help in this one area would release the backlog of getting paid in her business. In the ditch, thinking is put on hold so the many parts of you can preserve sanity. Irrational thinking leads to irrational decisions. A bookkeeper was not a 'nice to have'–it was a necessity, and it was more affordable than Christy originally thought.*
- ***Open all the overdue payment notices without judgment and organize these into a pile by company.** A primary reason why she was in the ditch to begin with–she created stories about what a loser she was and ran away from the growing stack of bills under her desk.*
- ***Begin to call each company and ask for help.** Each trip to the ditch brings a gift and Christy's was all about learning how to ask for help without feeling shame and guilt.*

True You Question

What purposeful actions can you take right now to lighten your load?

Connecting with God-Inspired Actions Take You to Higher Ground

When I first work with any client, one of the first questions I ask is, "What is trying to get your attention?" Usually there is one idea that repeatedly keeps coming to mind–usually in the car or during another purposeful activity–that would assist the person in going to higher ground.

Often, this 'idea' or 'flash of insight' is not practical and if it is handed over to the thinking mind will simply be tossed into the trash bin of 'that's nice, but I've got problems here to solve!' What you most need is always coming to you. The question is...*Are you listening?*

True You Question

What is something that keeps coming to mind that you have not acted on?

What calls to you during the ditch is levity and play. Right-brained activities such as coloring, drawing, re-decorating and spending time with friends beckon when the left-brain is overwhelmed. Many of us have been conditioned to ignore our own personal needs and to keep going. Take time for yourself and see what your *True You* has in store!

Planning for Healthy Distractions

Anyone who knows the old saying, "play hard, work hard" recognizes it is possible to do both. The idea of 'hard' is relative. I've observed that when people are in their work, loving what they do and loving who they do it for, working hard feels a whole lot different than when they are working hard doing work they despise for people who don't value what they do.

I like to think of it as play well, work well. Playing well can be the reward or the precursor for working well. As anyone who enjoys a great workout knows, feeling those muscles move, the sheen of sweat over their body, it is enjoyable to use one's potential. And so it is with meaningful play *and* work.

When clients begin, I want to know where they are in all areas of their life. What's working, what's not and what they are secretly wishing for or dreaming about?

When things aren't working, people tend to mentally check out and veer toward that darn ditch! It's the brain's default mode. It says, "I don't want to deal with pain, so I will ignore it." We check out in a variety of ways–a couple of beers or cocktails in the evening, a few hours in front of the "boob tube," several hours of mind-numbing video games, a pint of ice cream or any one of an endless variety of distractions.

I mention these because people will list these as their 'play.' When you look at my definition of 'play,' you'll soon see why they don't fit the bill.

Play, as I define it, is an intentional and deliberate choice to do something you *love*. It is not a diversion or a distraction from what you *don't* love, which just serves to divert your attention from what is not working. You are moving toward something, not running away from something. Play is adding something to and getting something tangible from the act of playing itself.

I have worked with several people who chose to play outside sports. They would swear up and down that they LOVED to play softball or they LOVED to run. However, when I asked, if you were a multimillionaire and you didn't have the job you have, would you still do it, each one said no.

After we talked about it, nearly every one recognized that they immersed themselves in these activities because they reminded them of high school or college when they were star athletes and they felt good about themselves. The truth was that they were miserable in their marriages, they were even more miserable in their jobs and these sports re-connected them to a happier time when they felt they were living their *True You*.

Sometimes play will show you what's missing, what could work even better, or the side of you that needs more attention. In the case of these men, they were in need of personal care and nurturing. Their jobs were demanding, their wives were demanding and they longed for a time when life was simpler.

Recognizing when an activity is a diversion and when it is play for play's sake is important. Think of it as the difference between shopping for clothes you love and being a shopaholic because you need to distract yourself from your reality. One enhances your life, and one makes your life more difficult.

One way to become aware of whether play is really play is to think about it in terms of enjoyment. Are you playing or participating in the activity for the sheer love of it, or does it define you? If it defines who you are, it is merely another mask to cover up the real you.

True You Questions

What is your favorite way to play?
Do you play because you love it or does it define you?
Is this your form of play or someone else's?

Play can contribute to effortlessly creating the life of your dreams. Play allows us to let go of the steering wheel for a short time. It allows us to trust God is at the helm. It puts us in a high frequency that matches all we dream about and want in the world. It literally is a gateway to receiving.

True You Tool

Play Dates

Since when did we outgrow having fun? One of my friends and I decided we were going to make play dates part of our life and business enhancement strategy. Every other month we take turns creatively planning and scheduling fun play dates. We are both women and have similar tastes in activities, so it is easy for us to be together. The first month we did this, we came back and, lo and behold, we both had new clients. The second month we did this, even more wonderful things happened in the days that followed. We began to set and make mini-play dates, for example, at the nail salon where we would both get a manicure and a pedicure while meeting for business.

I shared this with some of my clients who were in desperate need of playtime, but who also kept insisting they did not have time to play. I encouraged them to find a play partner so they would have an accomplice.

I was delighted to hear that they enjoyed similar success! Some came back with creative ideas for their businesses; others found new business in their email. Most importantly, each reported feeling better and more optimistic about life in general.

Here are some guidelines for setting up play dates–use these or create your own!

- **Schedule a date and time**. We start early in the morning and go until sundown!
- **Take turns planning.** Taking turns invites more fun.
- **Decide on a budget**. Play dates can be free or nearly free with creativity.
- **Create a theme.** This makes the date a lot of fun. We have worked with colors of crayons for inspiration, and even had a day of 'If I were 18 again!'
- **Work out the logistics.** Who drives? Who pays?
- **Honor each person's likes and dislikes**. Be adventurous and stretch without compromising serious dislikes.
- **Have fun!** Don't be too serious. It's called play for a reason. Don't be surprised if you are rusty at 'fun.' No judgment!
- **Completely UNPLUG**. No cell phones. No email. And, no rush to run back and work.
- **Give a little, gain a lot.** The details can take time, but are so worth it. For one play date, my friend created a CD for the day of favorite, inspirational songs. Not only did we breeze through the day, we floated on musical inspiration!

A Few Words About Procrastination

Ever cleaned your entire apartment before finals week in college? This is a great way to free up space so you have more room to ready your mind for all the facts you need to absorb.

Many people drag around the procrastinator label like an anchor. Or worse, use it to beat themselves to a pulp. They lament about how they procrastinate, procrastinate even more when they aren't sure if they are even procrastinating, and on it goes. This is a serious form of self-abuse. Chiding yourself about procrastinating is focusing on the problem. The only way out is to determine where you want to go from here.

Once you become mindful about what you are doing, you can kiss the whole procrastination scenario good-bye, including all the low feelings, like shame and guilt, which go with it. Procrastination can be a short ditch in disguise. It's bringing you what you need–Can you see that?

I want you to know that you are smart, and you *do* know what you need. If you are antsy and not focused, then you probably need to exercise or to simply get up and move around. Do you have too much on your mind? Give yourself permission to do what you need to do to free your mind. Write down what is going on for you right now. Dump your mind again.

And, please, PLEASE! give up the self-defeating labels. Remember, what is taking you away from you is communicating that it is time to give *yourself* some more attention. If your modus operandi is to 'get in the mood' to get moving, and it is working for you, then I say honor that!

Section II

Discovering Passion In The Present, a.k.a. You Really Are a Live Wire!

"It's amazing how easily we can deceive ourselves into thinking we are living when we actually are only thinking about living. We are happiest when we are most alive. When you feel unhappy, it is only because you think you are living your life when, in Truth, you are not thinking nor living."

-Tina Ferguson

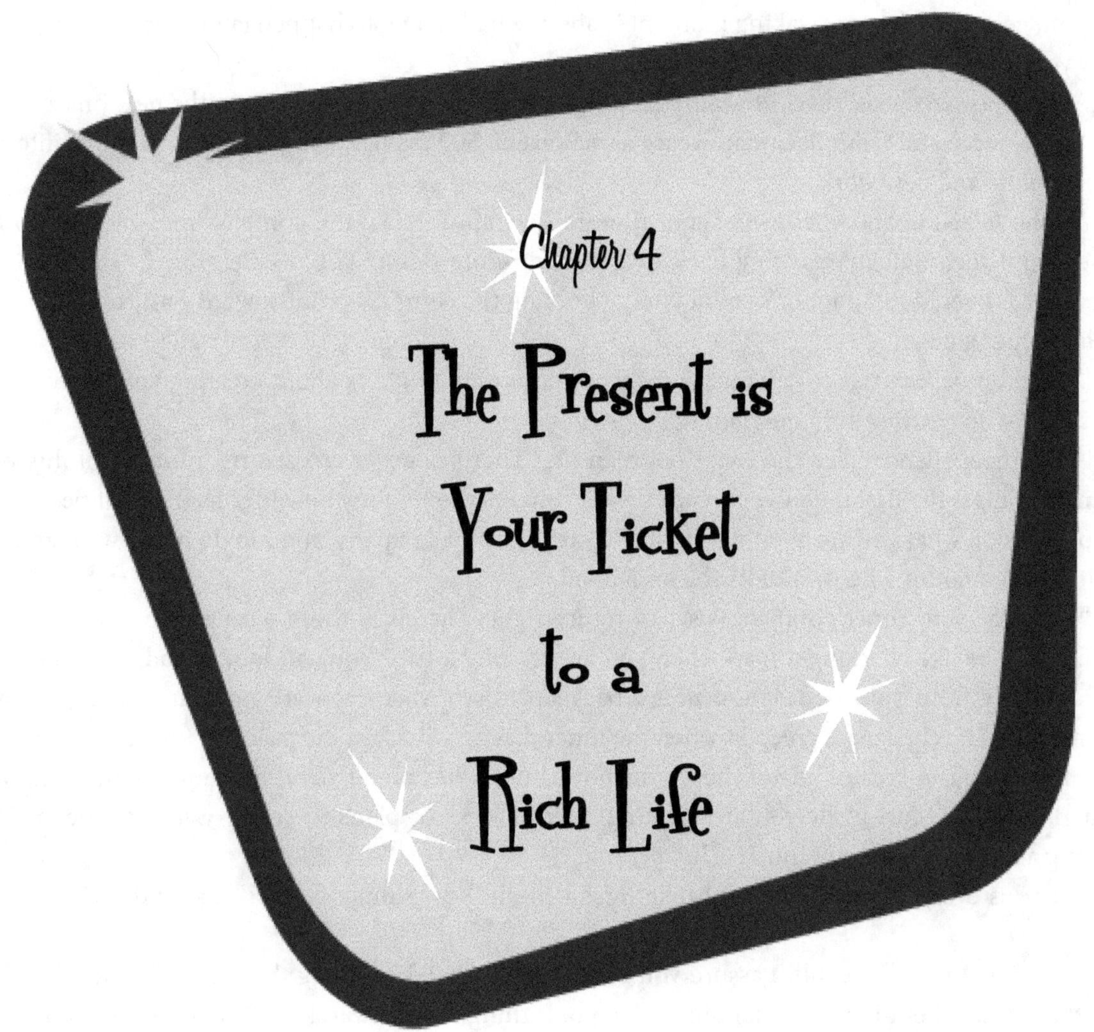

Chapter 4
The Present is Your Ticket to a Rich Life

"Each today, well-lived, makes yesterday a dream of happiness and each tomorrow a vision of hope. Look, therefore, to this one day, for it and it alone is life."

–Sanskrit Poem

"Behind the vision I had of the woman on the phone, I could see a compass. It appeared as if her photo was superimposed on top of it. Instead of N, S, E and W, I saw Future, Past, Current and Recent Past. Her compass appeared fixed on future. I saw the needle chaotically moving back and forth and then resting repeatedly on future.

"How much time do you believe you spend thinking about the future?" I asked.

"Oh, geez, almost every waking moment is about what's going to happen later today, tomorrow or a few years from now," she replied.

A high-powered executive, Jill wanted more than anything to get moving on the next phase of her life. Super-successful from her many years as a Fortune 500 trainer, she was eager to move into her life's purpose and new work.

As she talked about where she spent time in her mind, I saw the compass moving over to the present and then quickly resetting back over to the future point. The needle grew in size with her every word. I could feel a lot of mental energy holding the compass point toward Future. The energy felt like super glue.

"Would it be accurate to say that you spend more time *thinking* about creating your future than you actually do *creating* it?" I queried.

A pregnant silence filled the space between us. "That has never crossed my mind until this very moment. This is the first time I've thrown myself into envisioning my new life. That's what people say to do–envision what you are creating, right? Before, I just made up my mind to do it and went and did it. No wonder nothing has worked!" she exclaimed.

"I can see your inner compass is set to future sight. There's nothing wrong with that in and of itself. It can be like checking a map when you are starting a trip. You can look ahead to see how far you are away from your destination point, back up to see where you are now, and change course accordingly. The challenges creep in when the inner dial gets stuck in the past, the future or the recent past. Everything is created in the here and now, but if you aren't here and now, nothing new is created," I said. "Most likely you are creating a lot of ideas or plans to create–a lot of thoughts are swirling about, but likely not much is happening."

"Geez, is everyone you work with like this? I mean, how simple is this?" she said as if to scold herself.

"If it were that simple, Jill, I assure you more people would be living the life of their dreams in a way that brings them immense happiness. The best thing about awareness around where you are is that you get each new moment to shift your focus and attention. This is why the present is a gift that is available each and every moment!"

? True You Question

Past, Present, Future–Where Are You?

Where are you? Where is *your* compass needle pointed? Are you stuck in the past wondering why all of life's traumas made a recent appearance on your doorstep? Is your ex still driving you crazy after all these years? Do you worry about your future retirement? Write for a few minutes about what is on your mind. Where are you spending your time?

Your Attention Point is the Point of All Creation

Your attention point–your focus–is the point of all that you are creating. Some call it the 'now' or 'the present.' Whatever you call it, the only place where any of us ever create anything is right here, right now. Perhaps the hardest part of dealing with the 'now' is that often you want to either 'deal with the past' or 'plan for the future' inside of the present moment. Which, of course, keeps you from being present and creating something new! Throw on top of this that you likely often focus on what's going on now that you *don't* like instead of what we really want to create, and it can be a fun, silly experience that is very confusing.

When you are replaying tapes of the past or dreaming up visions of the future, you are in a place other than the here and now. As you develop your sense of self-awareness, one of the first things to do is to determine where you spend most of your time. Typically, people spend a majority of their time in one of four areas:

* Past
* Future
* Recent Past (a recent conversation, a recent upset, for example)
* Present/Current–Here and Now

Depending on what is going on in your life, your focus can change, and therefore where you 'are' changes. Much like the *Where's Waldo?* posters from a decade or so ago. This awareness is about knowing where *you* are. We all move easily back and forth between these stages, and there's nothing wrong with that. With practice, you can be more conscious and choose to be in the present more often. With presence, you life gets richer because more and more of your life moments yield what you choose.

However, when you begin spending too much time in some other space other than the here and now, your life begins to slide off the map. If you spend a great deal of time in the past, you will see yourself repeating the past over and over again. This is why it is important to gain new awareness of where your focus is–that's where you will find yourself and life.

True You Tool

Where do you spend most of your time?

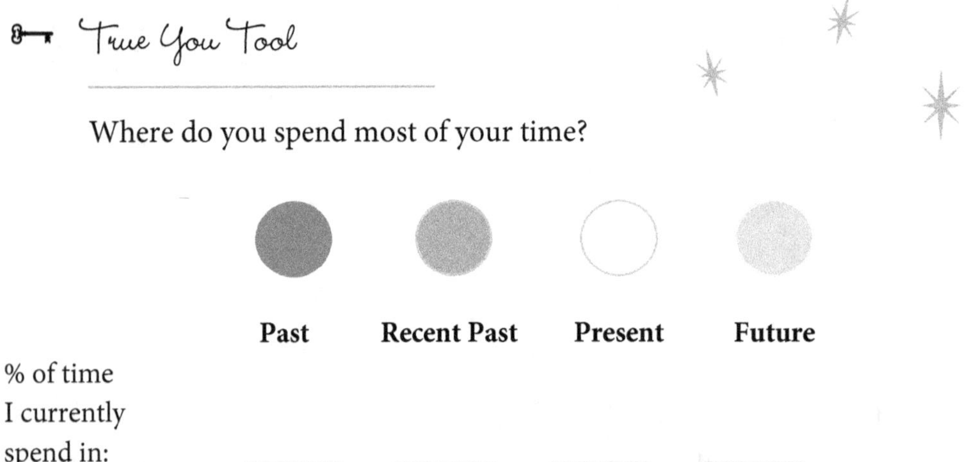

% of time
I currently
spend in: ______ ______ ______ ______

Go with the first thing that comes to your mind; what your intuition says is true for you. The total may or may not add up to 100 percent. Work with what you get. The intention is to draw attention to where you are spending most of your time. Allow that knowing, intuitive side of you to guide you. Your conscious mind does not have all the answers, I promise you this. If it did, then simply thinking about change would be enough. It is not. Self-awareness requires that you be intensely but gently honest with yourself (Heart Flash #7) about where your attention is and, therefore, where you are spending your priceless life moments. This seemingly small tool will reveal any energy that needs your attention.

I encourage you to work with yourself in a deeply intimate way as you build your new relationship with this amazing person that is your *True You*. In the last part of the program, we focused on getting out of the ditch and onto solid ground. Now we are preparing to plug you back into you. Note your thoughts here about 'where you are.'

Arrested Development

When you experience trauma, a mark is made on your body, mind and soul. Similar to a mark on the trunk of a tree that has endured drought or a storm, so too do you hold a mark on the parts of you.

If you are experiencing extreme fear or a paralyzing feeling toward something that is not life threatening, take a look at that area of your life and ask yourself, "How old am I right now in my career, health, relationship, etc.?" Trust the number that comes to you. This will indicate where you are in your emotional body. Go back to that age and ask yourself, "What was going on at that time in my life?"

These are not going to be memories you will need to find with a magnifying glass, these are emotional storms you have weathered, but where your development was stunted.

I see this a great deal in careers because people tend to hold onto a certain age when they *entered* the career and don't 'mature' within that area of themselves. I commonly see people acting 22 or 23–the age they left college–in their minds toward their bosses or clients when they are in their 40s, 50s and 60s with a lifetime of experience under their belt. To come back to the present, simply use the belief clearing process on page 77 to let go of your arrested development.

A woman named Gabriela was concerned about two things: the possibility of divorce and fear the business she really wanted to create would never get off the ground. We worked together because she felt immobilized by fear.

At first blush, these may appear to be future concerns–a future divorce or a future failure of a business. However, when we filled in the form, she responded that she was spending 75 percent of her time in the past, with 15 percent in the current and 10 percent in the future. Her focus was in the past because the fear that she was funneling came from memories entrenched in the past. The thought of a divorce immediately took her back to her first divorce with a small child when she struggled to make ends meet. It was a very stressful time. In addition, that time also was connected to the pain of financial problems. The final trek to the past revealed the pain associated with her religious faith, which did not condone divorce. Another divorce would make her a so-called two-time failure.

She may have been considering making changes for her future; however, she and where she was existing were planted firmly in the past. Because so much of 'her' was in the past, she couldn't access the present to **create** *her future. This was evident in the steps she could not and would not make due to fear. With the understanding of what was driving her anxiety, she could address it head-on. Her anxiety was real–very real–and this leftover energy from the past asked for her attention. Her ability to create her future was different from the situation being emotionally stirred up by the thought of change.*

Her future asked for her to first make peace with the energy inside that remained activated from the past. With this new awareness, she could honor the truth of that time, acknowledge herself for what she created during that time, upgrade her emotional body and finally come into the present to create from a place of personal power.

True You Tool

The Power of Forgiveness Meditation

Without a doubt, of all the tools have been given to me by Spirit, this is by far the most powerful one of all. This one tool can return love and joy to a heart overrun and riddled by shame, anger, hate and more.

For this meditation, sit in a comfortable chair or lie down. Take in a few deep breaths, deep into the lower part of your lungs so that your lower belly rises and falls. Relax your body starting from your feet or the top of your head, easily allowing each part of your body to relax.

Think of something you love deeply and unconditionally and allow this feeling of love to fill your entire body. Enjoy the feeling of love as it fills every cell in your body.

When you are ready, ask for every person who can be forgiven to appear. Do not be alarmed if you see a LOT of people in your mind's eye. This is an allowing, this is not a conscious exercise where you think about people or visualize people you want to forgive. Just allow the people who come into your mind to come to you. Your heart knows what is best. You can do this exercise one person by one person or you could do 100 people at once. Trust what feels right to you.

To begin the forgiveness process, focus on your chest where your heart is. Bring the feeling of unconditional love into your attention. See a luminous, shell pink cord coming out of your heart and connecting to the one or many people in front of you. The farther away the person appears indicates how much energy other than love is between you. None of this matters as this meditation resolves all energy between you and others.

When you are ready, send this feeling of unconditional love to the people to be forgiven. As you do this, the people will naturally move toward you in your mind's eye. A reminder: This is an allowing, not a visualization. Your role is to simply send the feelings and watch what happens. It all happens automatically. Let love unite you and all others.

When the person(s) are nose to nose with you, simply complete the forgiveness by saying, "I forgive you. I forgive myself. I love you. I love myself." You then will be complete with forgiving the individuals who came to you. And, you will see these people become one with you.

When you are complete, end by sending each person love and saying, "I return fully to myself in myself." This meditation works on the energetic level, so when it is complete, the forgiveness is complete and additional working out the details is often unnecessary. To check to see if you are completely neutral, think of the person or people you just forgave. You will not have any emotional residue if you are complete. If you feel any emotion toward the person other than neutrality or love, then simply repeat the forgiveness meditation.

When you have conflict with another person, you can use this to neutralize hurt feelings. If you find yourself thinking about a person or a conversation, you may need to do this three or four times over the course of a few days, but with commitment, this tool can easily shift you and eliminate hurt feelings.

This is a POWERFUL tool. Please use this meditation with care. I encourage you to use it on at least a monthly basis to release little hurts that accumulate through living everyday life. Even a person who cut you off in traffic can appear before you for forgiveness if you sent them a big pile of not nice thoughts. Please don't judge the reasons why, just simply tune into unconditional love and let go. Do not forget to come back to yourself and release your connection to those you have just forgiven. This is very important. If you would like to use a guided meditation, you can access this Forgiveness Meditation on my site at www.TinaFerguson.com.

Finally, you are the most important person to forgive. Remember to spend time with yourself in true unconditional love and forgiveness.

A Few Words About the Present

Volumes have been written about living in the present moment. I also call the 'here and now' the current because it is the place of flow. It is the place where you meet with your co-creators, with your higher self, with all possibility and opportunity. It works very much like a current in a swift-moving river–if you will allow it to move you.

Your dedication to understanding and expanding your self-awareness will reap exponential rewards. When you plug into the current of life–the source of all living–you will dance like an electric current. *You* will be a live wire!

Time Traveling From Past to Future—All You Get is Whiplash

If you imagined yourself looking left and then right and then left again over and over until you felt like your head was spinning, you would have a pretty good idea of what it is like to be focused on the future, then on the past, then on the future, then on the past. It is a crazy-making exercise of self-delusion. You literally are hiding in plain sight from the moment at hand.

A common experience where this appears is after a break-up or divorce. Let's say you are separated from your partner. You might think of the past and the good times you shared. Another thought may follow that finds you thinking of the future, the perfect future where none of the problems are present. Then reality sets in and you are back to the past. Then the future again. All you get is whiplash and motor mind from this back-and-forth travel. The fastest path out of this cycle is to make a decision. The following exercise can help you determine what that decision is.

The Recent Past–TiVo for Your Soul

The recent past allows us to reflect on events, on conversations we had, so we can take in the wisdom of our recent actions. The recent past is where we can go to gain access to energy that pulls our attention so we can make choices firmly in the present. Here and now, you can address your challenges and make peace with yourself. The recent past can enable you to work through what didn't work in an argument and perhaps throw around ideas of what would work in the future.

This is a rest stop for your mind to catch up to you–your body, your soul, your unconscious mind that has already taken everything in. It is a wonderful place to spend time each day to take out any garbage that may be lingering in the conscious mind such as, "What did he mean when he said that?" "Just exactly who does she think she is?" "Why did I do that?" and any other unanswered questions.

It is not a good place to stay if you are in the habit of beating yourself up over your performance, your appearance, or anything else. Go here, take what you need, and move back into the present to shift as you move forward. Use the Power of Forgiveness (page 57) to let go of any and all 'open items' for the day.

Time to Hit Pause

When you experience the back and forth motion of the time travel ocean, stop and ask:

- What do I really want in *this* moment?
- What can I take from the past that will heal me?
- What do I hope to get from what I am projecting into my future?
- What is the next inspired action to take?

What thoughts come to you now about what you desire?

True You Question

How do you spend your time?

Do you choose how you spend your time? How you spend your time reveals a great deal about you. Do you spend time doing things others want to do? Living in the recent past, thinking about how you could have spoken up or chosen to do something differently? Do you spend your time doing the things you love to do–enjoying the moment for all it has to offer you? Is your time spent in a way that reveals what is honored and revered, or is it poured all over the place as if it has no value? Do you make conscious decisions toward choices that lift you up, or do you float atop a choppy sea, open to the whims of others?

Life Priorities

Take a look at this list or use your own words to create your life's top priority list. Which areas do you want to spend your life-time doing?

* Adventure
* Beauty
* Career/Work
* Children
* Community/Social
* Dreams
* Education
* Family
* Finances
* Health/Exercise
* Hobbies
* Pet Project
* Pets
* Philanthropy
* Relationships
* Religion/Spirituality
* Self
* Self-expression– art, etc.
* Self-improvement
* Travel

The Five Areas I Value Most Are	Amount of Time I Spend Here Per Week
Example: *Health/Exercise*	Example: *2 hours*

Is there a gap between what you *think* you value and what you really spend your time doing? Note your thoughts here:

It's Never Too Late

Garry's Story

A client named Garry called one day because he was overwhelmed with a sense of loss about 'wasted time.' This feeling revealed itself when he said, "I wish the Creator would just take me now so I can start over and make better use of my time here."

At 52, he felt like half of his life was wasted with little more than a lot of material possessions to show for it. Like many people, he wanted his life to reflect significance. He used his age to sort out his ambivalence toward his true desire to leave a legacy in the world that would live long after him.

"Did you know that Mother Teresa didn't really get started with her primary charity until she was nearly 40?" I asked.

"What?" he replied, clearly amazed. "How is that possible?"

"It's true," I said. "People think she did all she did from a very early age, but she didn't. Plus, she was really afraid the first year after she left the convent. That year, she walked through poverty and began to see the lives of those she felt God called her to serve. She developed deep compassion for the poverty-stricken during that year."

"Wow, I didn't know that," he said with hope in his voice. "Still, I'm older," he added with a sigh.

"What is it you are most afraid of? Is it starting too late or not starting at all?"

The question surprised him, "I guess I just don't want to let God down. I feel like I've just wasted my life; I've chased the wrong things. I put money before God. I feel undeserving."

His self-consciousness pulled him away from his Truth. I knew what he really desired was to make a difference in many people's lives and to utilize his amazing people talents in a way that would bring glory to God. I asked how many people he thought he would touch in the first year of the new business he felt pulled to create.

"I would say 25 employees in each of 10 companies," he said. "250 for the year."

"Okay, so let's put some math to this," I said. "250 people who then, on a very small average, touch 100 other people when they are affected by your teachings. That makes 25,000 people you will touch this year, right?"

"Yes," he replied. "I suppose that's true," he said sounding intrigued at the idea of mathematically exploring the ripple effect.

"Okay, great. So, then let's say you touch 500 total people in your business next year, and that will make 50,000 people touched in one year. How many years do you think you might want to do this?"

"Well, I suppose since I enjoy it so much, I'll do it until I'm 65 or so," he replied.

"Perfect. Now remember, this is just simple math–I haven't taken into account how many people will be affected year after year from the changes in these people as they go out and live their greatness, and I haven't included the residual effect of each of the people touched and how they go on to touch other people. We are strictly looking at the actual participants who will go through your program. You

are 52 now, and for 12 years you are going to touch 50,000 people, right? When we add the 25,000 for the first year, it's 625,000 people touched. That's quite a few."

"It certainly is," he replied. "I didn't think of it in that way."

"And if you think about each of those people touching just half of the people the original participants touched, you can see that it grows and grows to well over a million people."

"I can see now that it's never too late," he said. "And, I've added so many skills in this life and I have so much more to offer now than I did when I was in my 30s."

Sometimes you are busy making a life that will blend easily into the life you happened to create. While it may not seem apparent to you, it is likely that you've been adding all kinds of tools to your tool belt that will serve you and your deepest dreams.

In all experiences, you are either moving toward something you desire or away from something you do not desire. Either way, your soul is always guiding you toward what you desire and who you really are. If you get enough of what you don't want, soon enough you will course correct and move toward what you do want.

It's better than you think, and more logical than you can imagine. You've been gathering an understanding, developing a strong relationship with yourself, so to speak. You know more today than you did years ago. There is no doubt a list of things you know you do *not* want to do, and probably a list equally as long of things you *love* to do.

Now is the time to focus on the list of things you would like to build your life around and to begin imagining a life full of these things.

I Lose Track of Time When I…	I Love To…	I'm Really Great At…	People Often Ask Me To…
Ex: *Write*	Ex: *Read novels*	Ex: *Telling a story*	Ex: *Speak at meetings*

Crystal Clear Clarity

Life Recap

* If I died tomorrow, I would be completely happy with the way I lived my life. T/F
* If false, what I would most regret is ______________________________.
* What's holding me back from this is ______________________________.
* Three ways I can incorporate this into my life (repeat this as many times as needed for different items):

____

____

____

Detours and Distractions

While you may be driving on Easy Street by now, there are a couple of detours you want to be aware of along your self-awareness path. An unexpected trip, a full-fledged sabotage crisis situation of your own making, a rescue of a sibling in need, a long trip to the ditch–detours come in many different shapes and sizes. Not all detours are bad. Most are loaded with great learning experiences. A detour can vary in length of time and severity–it all depends on you. Some may even argue that detours *are* part of your chosen path.

The key is to be aware when you are entering into one so you can choose whether you really want to take a detour. Some detours are absolutely supportive in our soul growth. Some are a reflection of our victim thoughts, our rescuer habits, and with practice of being aware of 'where you are' and understanding at various points in time what you are *really* seeking, you will begin to know yourself in a way that few do. By knowing yourself very well, you can gracefully float by the detour exit when it beckons–*if you choose to*. Soon, you will find that the queasy feeling in your tummy means you are scared. Scared of what? Scared of repeating the past? Oh, that? No problem!

Detours show up to take us off course both so we can grow into what is coming, and they show up to help us avoid growing. There's the light and the shadow–the true aspect and the counter-aspect. They work together as two sides of the same coin. We'll never be able to remove the counter-aspect. All parts are needed for our journey.

Remember, this is *your* story and you get to write the lines. Do you really need a two-year stint in an MBA program to validate to yourself (and others) that you are already a guru in your chosen profession? Is it important to follow your friends to another country for a cause *they* are passionate about? Only you know the Truth.

Remember that detours are marked with a decision to go. If you choose a detour, it is also up to you to determine what lessons your detour brought you. Some people find their lives are an endless string of detours. The victim mindset lends itself to staying on that off-ramp. You have choices. Decide for yourself.

Distractions are different from detours in that they are shorter-lived, and they usually accompany behaviors most of us call 'habits.' Distractions are a great way to remove yourself from what you really want to do in this moment. They can serve to keep you 'occupied' so you don't have to 'think' or be *aware* of what you aren't being. Distractions are the addictions and obsessions that allow us to 'check out' and disconnect for a moment, an hour, weeks or even months. Anything that is *driving* you is not the *True You*. Your soul is gentle like a river; it will never feel like you are being forced toward a goal.

Here's the catch, though. Once you know your distractions, your mind will never, ever work the same way where they are concerned. Suddenly, you have awareness around what you are unconsciously doing to distract yourself away from what you *truly* want. Once you open a can of worms, it can never be sealed again. Add to this that you are telling yourself only the Truth (Heart Flash #7) and you will be off and on your way to living in the present–in your Presence–a majority of the time!

Everyone has distractions. Distractions can sometimes be exactly what you *need*. The mind that is racing in two hundred directions at once *needs* the distraction of a bicycle ride. The key to working with your distractions is asking, "Is this taking me closer to what I most want or farther away from it?"

First Aid for Your Mind

No judgment here. This is about increasing your self-awareness so that next time you reach for a distraction, you are *choosing* it, in full awareness. Name your favorite distractions. If you've listed these in a previous chapter, skip this or add to your list.

These are the activities you use to make yourself feel better when:

* You don't know what to do or are overwhelmed.
* You feel alone or depressed.
* You feel scared or angry.
* You can't feel at all.

"I'm mad at you because now I can't just go distract myself anymore," Melanie whined. "I mean, I can't distract myself without guilt anymore."

"The point is not to feel bad; the point is to be at choice," I reassured her. "When you are distracting, what do you really want? What is it you are looking for? When you answer those questions, you'll find your answers–and what will ultimately be a lot more satisfying."

"I'm not really mad. I'm glad I'm not going in circles anymore. I just wish I knew what the next step is."

"That's your answer," I replied.

What is Your Vision Point?

Your focus is the laser beam in the center of your attention. If you gave the parts of your brain jobs, the conscious mind would be in charge of focus. Focus is the Vision Point. It is where you put the most concentrated part of your intention on a specific outcome. When you began driving a car, your entire focus was on driving. Now, likely, your focus is elsewhere–at least partially so–while driving.

Your attention is the unconscious mind's domain. It is the music in the background that is creating your reality. The two work together. One without the other is like a boat without a rudder; it pushes you to go in circles. Your unconscious mind follows your conscious mind's focus. It only knows how to agree and follow. This is why being aware of where you are is so vitally important.

Remember, your feelings indicate what your attention is. If you are feeling uneasy, likely there's something under the surface that requires your *conscious* attention. Your feelings may be pointing to other things under the surface. You can add to the Vision Point exercise below by focusing on your feelings and also asking, "What do you want me to know?" A question like this can help you access the feelings under the surface. Just simply go with whatever pops in your mind. Trust yourself. You know best and the *True You* is always guiding you home. Any feelings that don't feel good are an invitation to ask for a better feeling to replace it!

Crystal Clear Clarity

Your Vision Point

Today, most of the day, what has your conscious mind has been focused upon?

What I would rather be focused on is:

My focus tells me:

Your focus tells you a great deal about what you care about, what is important to you and what needs your conscious attention. The most important thing to remember is that your focal point is moving you toward your next creation point. Are you focused on slights others have put upon you? Do you want more of these? If not, change your Vision Point.

Chapter 5

Separating Fact From Fiction

"It ain't what you don't know that gets you into trouble. It's what you know for sure that just ain't so."

-Mark Twain

Geoff was a striking man with a relaxed grin that matched his laid-back personality. Well over six and a half feet tall, he commanded attention when he walked in a room. His charismatic, relaxed way reminded me of George Clooney. I had no idea what this young entrepreneur could be looking for when I met him. He was referred to me by a close family friend who had been trying to be a mentor to the young guy who wanted to 'do something more with his life.'

I asked him, "What is it you most want right now?"

"I want to have my own business, work less and spend more time with my family," he replied.

Although I could feel that he didn't believe he actually could have the things flowing from his mouth, I didn't address it. Instead, I focused on helping him understand what was coming in between himself and the Truth. "So, what's keeping you from having that?"

"I don't have any money," he quickly replied. This was the first belief standing between him and his dreams. His limiting belief was that he had to have money to get started.

"What does money have to do with anything?" I asked.

"Well, you have to have seed money to get a business started. You have to have things like business cards."

He had another belief–you can't be in business without business cards. This one is a form of rules–"Others have business cards and I need them, too."

"What if I told you that what you believe is not true?" I ventured. "What if I gave you several examples of people who are in business who didn't have any of these things when they got started, and were still successful?"

"I wouldn't believe you," he said confidently.

"Of course you won't. That's because you believe your beliefs are valid. You look to the world to validate your beliefs, but I am here saying I can also look to the world and know that your beliefs are not valid. I'm not saying these things are not important, I'm only saying that you can start with what you have."

"So, what is the point?" he asked.

"This is the point. Are your beliefs moving you forward or keeping you back?" I asked knowing we were pushing on the small part of him that didn't believe in something greater than his current experiences.

"I suppose they are holding me back," he reluctantly agreed.

"Are you ready to get out of the box? Do you really want all that you are saying you want? Or do you want to spend more time thinking about whether or not it is what you want, why you can't have it or a host of others things?"

"No, I'm ready," he said resolutely.

"Okay, let's go. What is the first step you can take?"

"I guess I could start to look at business opportunities to figure out which one I like."

"How much does that cost?" I asked.

"Nothing," he laughed, "I'm getting your point."

"Let's say you find an amazing opportunity that is going to cost you $1,500 to get in on. What are you going to do?"

"Figure out a way to get $1,500, probably," he responded.

"Yes, that's right. Do you know why you would do that instead of saying 'I don't have any money?'"

"That didn't occur to me," he replied.

"This is because you are focused on the creation, not on the idea of it. There's a different energy, a different feeling, a different way you approach something you are "going" to do versus what you are "thinking" about doing. Does this make sense?"

"Well, it makes a lot of sense. I don't know why I didn't see that before."

"It matters less why and more that you allow yourself to go forward and do it," I reassured him.

"But I don't have any experience running a business," he replied.

This is another belief–the belief is *I can't run a business unless I know how.* I pressed again so he could recognize it as a belief or a rule.

"What does that have to do with anything?"

"Well, what if I mess it up?" he shot back.

His fear revealed itself. ***What if I fail?***

"Okay, I'm going to ask you a quick question and I want you to tell me the first three things that come to your mind."

"Okay, shoot."

"What are three things you know how to do now that you used to not know how to do?"

"Very funny. I get it. I'll go with it. Ride a bike, program a computer, be a parent."

"Great. These are really different. When you decided to become a parent, did you stop because you'd never been a parent before?"

"No. Of course not," he laughed again. "Once the bun is in the oven, you are pretty much committed to the goods."

"And what happens when you don't know how to parent or don't know how to work with your kids?"

"I figure it out–the faster the better," he replied laughing harder.

"So, would it be truthful to say you are a fast learner?"

"Yes. Yes, it would," he said more confidently.

"Would it be possible that you could learn just as fast about business as you have about parenting? Or learn to find others who know even more than you do?"

"Okay, I see your point. But, if I screw up the business, I could lose my money!"

His fear surrounding money showed up in both his current lack of it and in his fears of losing any money he might gain. Unless something changed within him, he would be caught in circular logic.

"What happens if you screw up with your kid? What happens then?" I asked, staying with his Truth.

"I fix it fast and find the answer," he said, laughing harder now.

"The same thing happens in your business. You have an experience; you back up and say, 'Was this good? Should I do more of this? Or, was this bad? Should I not do this again or get another way of doing it?' Life is really pretty simple–it's our reactions to things that make it more complex."

"You make it sound so easy," he sighed.

"It is easy when you realize that when you are focused on what you want, the opportunities are going to come to you, and it is truly your job to get out of your own way so you can fly."

Beliefs, Rules and Baggage

Ready to fly? Is it time to reduce a 42-piece luggage set down to a carry-on bag of beliefs? When you begin revealing the *True You*, beliefs will meet you at the door of your mind. Any rules you are operating under will appear, too. Certainly, the fears, worries and concerns stowed away in your baggage will crop up as well.

In this example, several beliefs came to the surface when Geoff started really looking at what he wanted to create. When you see these markers along the road, consider them happy reminders that you are moving into your Truth.

Until you make a decision to go your own way, any thoughts or ideas you may have are just that–a series of thoughts rolling around in the ether in your head. The energy of 'thinking about' something is tremendously different from the energy of 'creating' something.

The energy of creating, combined with deliberate action, can sweep away the limiting beliefs, dismantle outdated rules and empty any lingering stories (baggage).

True You Tool

Baggage Clearing

We all have it. Some of us travel with a sleek carry-on and some of us have a 42-piece matching set of luggage. No judgment here. Just know that we all have some, and that the sooner we clear it, the easier it is to be who we truly are.

The easiest way to find your baggage is to think of all the ways you are insulted, outraged, offended, defended, offensive, defensive, protective and frustrated in a day. These seemingly innocuous hurts will point right to your baggage.

List them here:

As you begin to think about living your life fully, what beliefs pop up telling you it isn't possible or it's too hard? You can use your thoughts from the last chapter. Like Geoff's example, you can begin to see the ideas that keep you from trying. Record them here. Then take those and shift them so they are supporting beliefs.

Beliefs Holding Me Back	Beliefs Supporting Me
Example: *I'm not smart enough.*	Example: *I am capable of being successful.*

A Personal Story From the Queen of Dreams

For most of my life, I had this compulsive need to always have one or two 'extra' of everything in the house. That meant I wanted an extra deodorant, extra bars of soap, extra toilet paper rolls, extra paper towels. I also wanted to fill the gas tank to FULL every time it was empty or nearly empty. I knew that this seemingly silly tic was something bigger when I got really upset one day when my husband took my car and only filled it up halfway.

A belief that is resulting in behavior that isn't working is one that needs to go. When I followed the steps above, I found my belief stemmed from my childhood, when I lived with my grandmother who grew up in the depression and feared lacking the things she needed. Her habit, as a result, was to always buy extra for everything.

My little girl mind took this in as, "We are safe when we buy more and are sure we have enough." As I grew older, when I perceived I didn't have enough, it turned into uneasiness and a feeling of lack. I would get so upset when I would reach for a bar of soap and find that I didn't have one.

The difference between an inconvenience and a belief that is out of line is the amount of feeling behind it. If it feels or seems irrational, it probably is an outgrown belief. In my case, the 'Truth' of the situation is that my grandmother was just following a pattern she created when she was a child, and I was just following along. When I saw that I could choose to know that when I needed something, I could simply just go to the store and get it, I could release this belief for a healthier mindset.

Now, if I run out of deodorant or soap, it is inconvenient, but it isn't emotional. It sounds like a small thing, but when you take a look at your list, soon you will see how a few of these little things can really wreak havoc on your life–and your relationships. ♥

Rules You Live By That Are Not Your Own

Are you living by someone else's rules? Is it time to step to the beat of your own drum? It's time to let go of outdated rules! Rules accompany words like must, have to, need to and should.

When you bump up against your baggage (a.k.a. fears, worries, beliefs), ask yourself:

- Is it true?
- What can I learn from the Truth?
- What is this here to teach me?
- What do I choose to believe?
- What's my next step? What can I do now?

Changing is not easy work, but it's work that can be easy if you will allow the changes to guide you. To let go of the baggage and beliefs that are not yours, you'll need to let them appear so you can begin sifting through what you want to keep and what you want to let go. With this, it will be much easier to dump the trash!

Mastering New Beliefs

You've been living with your beliefs for a long, long time. "I can't..." "I couldn't..." "That won't work for me..." "This is too easy..." "This is too hard..." "It can't happen..." "I won't..." "I've done that before, but that didn't work for me..." on and on it goes. To free the *True You*, you want to get out of here (which isn't even real, by the way–this is an imaginary box created by you):

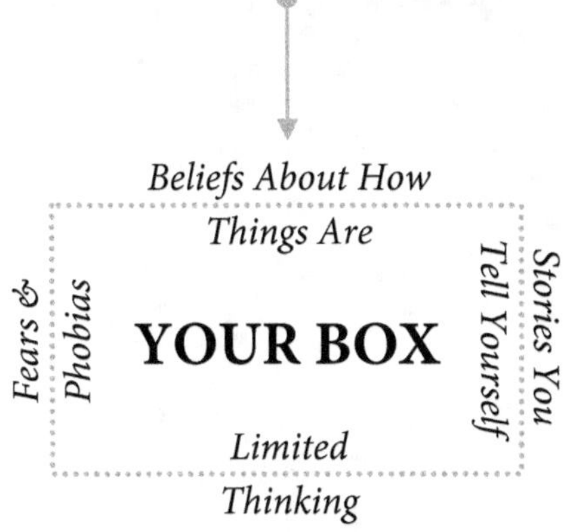

You are the master of the box you have created. The box is built by the beliefs you've accepted up to this moment, the fears you've stored, the stories you've woven and the limited thinking you are working under. If you want to move out of the box where you currently reside, you will be required to rethink some beliefs and consider some new ways of thinking.

When I work with clients, part of what we do is identify what is working against what they most want to create. We begin with pretending that you don't know anything. This can peel back layers and layers of ideas of how things *must* work. Yes, life can be predictable, but you really never *know* until you get to the moment and find out how the story plays out.

True You Tool

The Power of Acceptance

Make a list of things you don't like about how you act or the way you are with others. For example, if you are impatient with your friends or family and you don't like it, put impatience in a box below. However, don't add it if you are fine with your impatience. Only add to the list the things that *bother* you, pull your attention and bring up bad feelings within yourself.

The Power of Acceptance is about accepting yourself just as you are, exactly where you are. The part of you that is resisting you keeps you from your power. Don't judge yourself during this, and please give yourself the space to really get everything down. This can be like writing a grocery list...unemotional. This is a laundry list of all the things you think you need to change about yourself. This exercise is simply about letting go of the attachments you have to your own judgments about yourself. All of us have occasions where we have an outburst, lose our cool or don't speak up when we want to. That's completely normal. When these occasions happen more often and they affect your self-image, that's another issue altogether. Write your list here:

This is an opportunity to clear out the junk beliefs that have been influencing the way you act and interact with the world at large. Complete the list at your leisure. After making your list, work through the issues as you feel ready to do so. Some people tackle a few in a month. Some work on many at once. Some try half and half. This is highly personal and releases a lot of energy at deep levels, so do it at your own pace.

You can address each one easily and simply accept it. For example: It's okay to be messy. It's okay to be talkative. It's okay to be...and on you go accepting each one of the things that you thought was not acceptable before. For those that have more emotion or are not easily accepted, use the following process to make peace with and accept this part of yourself.

Follow these steps as you address each belief:

1. Take a deep breath and focus on the area behind your belly button.
2. Allow a white light to appear and see it getting larger and larger until it fills up your body shape.
3. Pull the center of this spark up into your heart.
4. Put your left hand over your belly button and your right hand over your heart.
5. Ask your heart to take you to the origination of this belief, habit or block.
6. You may see a little movie in your imagination or a memory may come to mind.
7. When you know the origination, ask yourself, "What did I choose to believe in this moment?"
8. "What is the bigger picture perspective in this moment?"–This will be at a Higher Self level–an understanding that comes from you about what was *really* happening at the time.
9. Ask yourself, "What is the Truth of this experience? How did this serve me?"

10. When you have the Truth and can also see the gift in what you have been carrying, you can now choose and replace this with a new Truth.
11. Sometimes, our experiences birth new beliefs. By working with your heart, you bypass the mind's 'logic' and go straight for the root of the limiting belief. However, sometimes we go back to a moment that is not the origin. In this case, we simply ask, "Is there anything else I need to acknowledge to let this go?" If the answer is yes, then you will find yourself in another memory.
12. Listen to the answer. Then follow it to the origination point and start again at #7.

Usually, you will only go back to one or two moments. If you are dredging up lots of memories, then you want to go back and connect to your heart again. The mind does not hold your answers–it holds the stories. You can also use the Connect to Love (page 11) tool to deepen your heart connection. This is less about thinking and more about allowing and connecting to your soul's Truth.

This is a super simple way to laser in on things that pull you down in the moment, too. It takes effort, of course, as does everything worthwhile. Remember, use this process above for the beliefs that hold a lot of emotion for you. For all the others, simply write for each one: It is okay to be and enter the item. By surrendering what you want to run away from, these things can lose their potent effect on you.

These tools provide assistance when you are in the moment and find yourself stuck. Focusing too much on clearing and the other tools can turn into a new obsession. Be sure to focus on living the life of your dreams!

A Personal Story from The Queen of Dreams

I remember when I first learned this process. Spirit messengers brought this to me and walked me through one belief after another. I spent months releasing myself belief by belief from the prison I had erected around me. In the years since I have stepped into more of my True You, I have had more opportunities to embrace more of what is true while at the same time letting go of what isn't.

Today, it doesn't seem nearly as hard or as big as it did at the beginning, and yet the stretches between bumping into these beliefs get longer and longer. It's all good.

I do also remember back in my early 20s facing the thought of dealing with my thoughts. I told myself, "I can't do that." And, I didn't for another 12 years. I believe my soul was already ready, but I still had a lot of learning to do around how to deal with my smart, overly active strategic mind. Thank goodness God doesn't ever give up on us. Still, I would encourage you to ***start today****...allow your heart to lead you.*

The Holy Grail of Limiting Beliefs–Major Blocks

A major block has the potential to hold you back from moving forward. If you want to do something and you just can't seem to get yourself going, there is likely a major block of some sort. I have noticed that if people can keep moving forward–no matter what the pace–they can achieve their goals and dreams while at the same time connecting to the Truth within.

Major blocks can assume many forms. This section is designed to help you know yourself intimately so you can understand the inner workings of your mind and soul. The more that you know what is driving and affecting you, the more power you have to determine for yourself and choose for yourself what you want.

Perhaps the easiest way to determine a major block is to look at what is keeping you from moving. What is stopping you? What fears come up when you think of achieving your dreams? What stops you in your tracks? What does that little inner voice whisper when you write your perfect day? What is that one thing that stands between you and your dreams? You know what it is.

These are different from the beliefs that cause us to act in ways we don't like. These actually stop us in our tracks. These are the biggies that keep us from living in our full potential.

The best way to overcome fear is to call it. Just put it out there and be done with it. When you pull those fears out into the light of day, they have a way of shrinking. Those shadows move from being monsters to something you can deal with.

Facing & Disarming Fear

Paul's Story

I remember working with a client who felt 'less than' because he didn't have a degree. Never mind that he was an amazing businessman and sharp as a tack. He helped companies increase profits, and yet he was left with a feeling that he couldn't compete with others. Regardless of the results he helped his clients achieve, regardless of his impressive list of clients, he couldn't shake the feeling that he just didn't belong.

I suggested he face his fears and put them front and center. In his marketing materials, he used his biggest fear–the fact that he didn't have a degree and the thing he was most afraid of people finding out–as his biggest differentiator and a way of setting himself apart from other companies. It was an instant success. Suddenly, people wanted to know how this guy with no degree and no industry experience could know so much about their industries. His Achilles heel was now his ace in the hole. By putting his fear front and center, he disarmed it and moved past it as he walked in his Truth.

When I work with clients, I get an intuitive feeling when they talk about their fears. The energy feels like it is hiding. When I follow it, I usually see the person and some representation of what they are trying to hold in their closet. Sometimes, it feels like a closet that is bursting at the seams and they are using all their might to keep it locked away.

All that mental effort to work 'around' what isn't even real robs you of energy and mental acuity that could be better used for something useful. I haven't seen one person's fear where I couldn't find a success story where a person shared the same characteristic or experience. The difference between people who successfully embrace life and those who spend way too much time in the ditch is how the person manages his or her fears and faith.

Successful people have created habits and techniques that allow them to take action despite blocks and fears. As they walk through the fear, they begin to feel less fear–they transmute the fear. With people who don't have such supportive habits, they get through one fear and think it was a 'lucky break,' which means the fear never goes away. My hope is that this book will help you see every part of you as a gift–including your fear–so you can truly remember all that you are. Connected people go forward with a knowing that things *will* happen. They have faith in themselves, faith in God and they know that if they keep going, things will happen. This is a different type of energy–it isn't the energy of 'I'll try' or 'we'll see'–it is the energy of *connection.*

These examples are people who, just *like you,* once had a dream to be themselves and to be successful. Each just went and trusted. You can do this too!

Fear	Success Stories
I don't have the education or credentials.	Tony Robbins didn't have a degree or credentials in his industry when his career took off.
I don't have the image, correct body weight, clothes, etc.	Oprah was the so-called wrong size, the wrong color and wasn't the stereotypical talk-show host when she took over her time slot on daily television, knocking off talk-show veteran, Phil Donahue.
I'm not smart enough, don't have the skills, etc.	Each year immigrants come to the United States not knowing the language, barely understanding our country. Many of them build very successful businesses in a short period of time.
I have no money or opportunity.	Farrah Gray walked door-to-door selling rocks as a child. Little by little, he added to his sales arsenal and made his first million by the age of 14 without one dollar of capital.
Who am I to be successful and wealthy?	Mother Teresa knew that to help many people, money was needed, but she didn't make her focus *about* the money. She focused on serving and her charities raised millions and millions of dollars.

Fear	Success Stories
I'm too old.	Mary Kay created what would become her mega company at 60. Zig Ziglar turned his life around at 45. Paula Deen started betting on herself at 42.
I'm not the best at ________________.	Robert Kiyosaki admits not being a best-writing author, but he is a best-selling author because his information feeds a hungry target market.
I'm not from the right background.	You are exactly in the right place to be all you were born to be. More first-generation successes exist today than ever before.

Your Biggest Fears

If you find yourself focusing on fears, use this section to let them out. This tool can help you neutralize the energy and fears in your mind. Record your biggest fears here.

Fear	What Do I Believe?	What is The Truth?
Ex: *I can't make it.*	Ex: *Following my dreams will take too long.*	Ex: *The longer I wait to start, the longer it will take.*

Storytelling: The Stories We Tell Ourselves

You've agreed to live by the Heart Flashes. To do this, you must claim responsibility for yourself (Heart Flash #2), your thoughts, your words and your actions. If you are responsible–truly responsible for yourself–you realize that you are the creator of your story. If you are responsible, truly responsible for yourself, you won't find yourself blaming others for your experience. It's impossible to do both at the same time.

If you are trying to lose weight, you choose what you put in your mouth. It doesn't matter what your spouse buys that is tempting, *you* put the food in your mouth. Begin to be honest with yourself regarding every choice you make–are you creating what you want or not?

What do your stories reveal about what you are telling yourself? "My boyfriend made me ___________." "My girlfriend forced me to _______________." "My mother ruins my life!" "My father is creating havoc in my marriage!"

These may sound like the victim because they do shift responsibility to someone else. The most destructive lies are the stories created to comfort us in the moment. These stories call for you to lie to yourself and then weave a tale so you can feel good. When you strengthen your inner core and can courageously look at the Truth without shaking in your boots, the need to weave tales to soothe your ego subsides. Just imagine how much more living you can do with the time you won't be using to tell tales! What are you going to do with all of that time?

What exactly is storytelling? It starts innocently enough. Your feelings are hurt. A remark at work ignites a flurry of "I'm not good enough" inside of you. Suddenly, your mind is busy. You want to feel better, don't you? Soon, a story unfolds in one of two directions. First, you may be putting the person in his or her place so you can dismiss the remark. Second, you may take the remark and use it to beat yourself over the head–repeatedly.

Crystal Clear Clarity

Your Favorite Stories

The fairytale(s) or story(ies) that you most closely resonate with is (are):

In this story, I am the:

I sometimes play other roles, including:

By identifying your favorite stories, you can simply be aware of the roles you play. When you are conscious of these, you can easily see and choose who you will be.

The victim orientation is mightily alluring, although it is ineffective when it comes to living big and free. If you are not taking responsibility for yourself, you are in the victim orientation of being put upon, where people do things to you and nothing goes your way. It is impossible to be a victim and a creator at the same time. If external things are being 'done' to you, then you are in the mode of 'helpless.' When you switch over to the place of knowing that you create what you are experiencing through your choices in full responsibility, it is difficult to deceive yourself.

For those of you who work with the role of Cinderella or Snow White, you might find yourself responsible for everyone else and not at all responsible for yourself. Take the opportunity to go deeper into understanding *why* you like to distract yourself with other people's problems. You may simply not even be aware you are doing this. Or, you might reveal how it sometimes seems easier to take responsibility for others' lives than it is to be honest and address your own life. If you take responsibility for others, then you won't have time to deal with yourself, right?

But, here's the catch. At some point, you will have to address full responsibility to move over to living the life you dream of. When you see that rescuing, taking responsibility for others, distracting yourself from your life and building a clock tower of stories to keep you safe and sound are just poor excuses for not living *your* life, it becomes easier to notice when you are out of balance with the *True You.*

If handling all this Truth seems insurmountable, think again. This is the road to the freedom *you are searching for.* When we live vicariously through the feelings of others, the experiences of others, the dreams of others, it takes us out of our own living.

The great news is that most, if not all of this, is habit. You may be in the habit of rescuing others who are 'not as fortunate' as you are. You may be in the habit of supporting the dreams of everyone you know, but not letting yourself dream big. You may even be in the habit of being the 'answer' for everyone you know even though when they leave you feel like a fake because you don't have the answers for yourself.

You may be to the right or to the left, a little more or less in this…but it doesn't really matter. The direction here is forward. Fast forward, as fast as you like.

The victim or helpless mindset is about telling yourself stories that keep you seemingly safe (see page 106 for *Say Goodbye to the Victim Mindset* tool). However, this program is built upon gentle honesty with yourself. You are a bold being, so there's no need to tip-toe around your weak ego or spare yourself the Truth. Those stories are set up to keep you from *feeling* the Truth, from *seeing* the Truth and *creating* from your Truth. They keep you in the closet, wasting away on stale Cheetos®, wishing you could be something more–the *True You.*

Truthtelling

Instead of going to storytelling, go to Truthtelling and begin to feel the feelings. Creating stories is a way to deflect the pain we face. Admit the Truth. Your feelings are hurt. That wasn't so bad, was it? From there, what hurts? Your ego? A reminder of a painful past? Find out what it is and then make peace with it using The Power of Forgiveness (page 57). When you go to Truthtelling instead of using storytelling, you create more space and connect to the love you are instead of running away from yourself. You are way too fun to run away from!

Note any thoughts you have about telling yourself stories and concerns about telling the Truth:

Right Here, Right Now

Your Story, Starring ____________________

Next, let's take a look at your current 'story.' Your story can reveal a lot of things you believe about yourself and what you can shift to support your new desires and outcomes. Let go of writing the story you think is acceptable and write down the story you carry around with you.

What are the key stories you share when you meet someone? What are the wounds you hold onto? How do you currently define yourself with your story? What does your story say about you? When you decide to embrace all you are and go to the next level, you must have the courage to face the story that has protected you for so long. Before you can release the story, you must acknowledge that it exists. Take some time for this–remember, what you resist will persist. You deserve to take time for this.

Facing the Truth

Mike's Story

I always thought I was pretty happy with my life. Things always seemed to just work out for me. I was captain of the football team. I married the head cheerleader. I have always been successful in sales, and for the most part, things just kind of go 'my way.' When I wrote my story, I realized that I feel like a phony. I don't try any harder than I have to. I just kind of go with the flow and just take what I'm given, which is more than I feel I deserve. There's a part of me that knows I am capable of a whole lot more, but I don't care enough to try.

I just keep living the role I was handed in high school where I was the envy of everyone in my class. I didn't ask for that, but that's what I got, and ever since then I've been living the life of 'that guy' that everyone wants to be. With this, all of a sudden, I thought, 'Who is 'that guy?' I just go through the motions, acting like everything is great. I think I've been in this mode since my dad left my mom, my brother and me. I put on the game face and got to work. Now, I'm 50, and I'm feeling like there's got to be more to life than this. It doesn't mean I don't love my kids or my wife, it just means that I feel like there's so much more out there waiting for me. I realize that I haven't been choosing at all–I've just been going with whatever everyone else wants.

When you adopted each part of the story you wrote, each piece held a role. One part may have been the protector, another may have been the hero, yet another may have been the persecutor. Take a look at your story and see the Truth in it now.

Part of My Story	How It Helped Me	The Truth Today
Ex: *Hero who helps everyone.*	Ex: *Gave me focus when I was sad and lost after dad's death.*	Ex: *I don't always have to be in the lead. Others can help me too.*

Making peace with your story is critical to a full connection with your *True You*. Your stories are like security blankets that wrap around you and make things 'okay.' I have a story; therefore, I am.

Here's the catch: Like yellowed photos, stories are often pictures of the past. You will never eliminate all your stories–Who would want to? We are most interested in the areas of your story that you use to define yourself today that are actually outdated and not in alignment with your soul.

In this old story, watch for disconnects in the ideas that do not support who you are and what you most want to share with the world. Honesty is the best policy here; share what you feel is your Truth. Are you a superstar who just hasn't caught a lucky break, is it always someone else's fault, do you feel like you have to do everything, are you the hero, are you the victim? What exactly is *your* story?

A Sparkling Tale From the Queen of Dreams

My husband and I once met a woman at a conference. Within minutes, she was sharing all the details of her life. Her mother passed when she was very young. She was always 'on her own.' She was alone, she said. It's okay, I choose to be alone she tried to tell us–even sell us on her story. In the course of perhaps five minutes, she must've said, 'I'm alone' at least 15 times. Every area of her life centered on this theme.

When the hostess came to seat us, and asked how many in your party, the woman replied, "Oh, I'm alone." We said, "No, you aren't alone, please join us. Unless you really want to be alone." We all laughed at how funny it was to say alone, alone, alone. Once we were seated, she shared many other stories about how people were not there for her and how she felt so alone. I asked her about what she really wanted. She told us that she really liked being alone. But when we asked her what she dreamed of…being alone was not at all what she wanted. ♥

Right Here, Right Now

Remembering Your *True You* Story

Now, let's write your story from the perspective of the *True You*. This is the life *you* are creating. You are remembering you. The person you are deep inside, the relationships you love and the perfect place called your life. Some of my clients write this story as a 'day in the life,' while others describe what they see in their dreams. Connect to the Love You Are (page 11) and then write what feels true for you. There are no rules here–this is your life–you create it!

In my story, I am…

True You Tool

Shine the Light of Truth—Ask Good Questions

Often, the stories we tell ourselves involve other people who have no idea they are in our stories. If you are making up stories throughout the day, remember to use some of the tools shared in this chapter to "shine the light of Truth" on the story.

- Is it true?
- If I don't know if it is true, do I need to know it is true?
- Can I let it go?
- What do I really want to know?

* What can I learn from the Truth that is here? What is this here to teach me?
* What do I choose to believe about this?
* What's my next step?

Asking why and how is like opening up the critic inside..."Why did I do this?" "How could I believe this?" Those questions take you down a long and slippery slope. Stay with the questions above and leave the word "why" and "how" out of your line of questioning. Why can reduce us down to five years old in five seconds flat–the fewer whys you include, the easier it is to keep judgment at bay.

A Word About Judgment

With all of the contests like American Idol on television, practically everyone has become a home expert on all things. To relax the judger inside of you, quit judging. Take a holiday from judging and notice how much lighter and happier you feel.

Judging, for some people, is a spectator sport. "Did you see what she was wearing?" "What is up with that car?" From something that looks innocent to a constant barrage of non-stop judgments about what is, judging can deliver you smack in the middle of the land of critical judgment. Even to call a rose beautiful is to judge it. Judging is a habit for most people. Usually you pick this up from your parents. And, it's never too late to change your habits!

By interacting with the world through this part of your mind, you miss the *experience* of what you are interacting with. Feel the rose instead of labeling it. Feel the experience of sitting next to your partner. How do *you* feel? How does the *other person* feel? Enjoy the connection!

Tracy's Story

I once worked with a guy who was paranoid. That's the reason he called me. His paranoia literally was taking over his life. He tried just about everything to get over his feeling that everyone was against him. When he called, we chatted for a few minutes and soon I could see images that showed me what his concern was. I saw him as a young boy and I saw two other boys telling stories about him at school. I could see them pointing and laughing, and I could feel this child's pain in my heart and stomach. From this experience, he developed an almost crippling fear of people talking behind his back.

When I asked him about what I saw, I felt he was almost tempted to say I must have researched him and found out things no one knew about. But the Truth shined brightly as he realized there was no way for me to know this information. Soon, he was in tears, talking about how awful the experience was. He was a gay man, and at the time, he was a very confused little boy. These boys took a traumatic time and made it worse by sharing their suspicions with his classmates.

As we worked with this tool, he began to breathe easier. One by one, we dismantled the lies, the stories he created to keep himself safe. One by one, he asked himself, "How do I know this is true?" Then he would answer, "I don't." "Do I need to know if it is true?" "No, I can let it go." For nearly an hour, we unraveled the mental energetic cords that held him captive.

The last time I spoke to him, he was doing fine and was in a new relationship. His paranoia was only a token artifact of his memory.

Taking responsibility for your life may seem like a lot of work when you begin using these tools, but I ask you to consider how much work it is to deal with a mind that is riddled with insecurity and chaos. With just a little bit of attention, you will be the master of your mind, body *and* soul. I am amazed at how a lifetime of shame or guilt can be erased in as little as an hour by looking deep inside into the love–into the light–of the *True You.*

Get Out of the Drama–Lucy TV

One of the most potent ways you can separate fact from fiction is to simply step out of the fiction. In the '50s sitcom, *I Love Lucy,* the show's main character, Lucy, is completely wrapped up in her drama. As the audience, we get to tag along seeing the big picture and watching poor Lucy dealing with the messes she gets herself into based on perceptions, half-truths, overheard whispers and any number of creative ways to get herself in a pinch.

Our own lives can resemble Lucy's TV life when we get too invested in the drama day to day. Are you reacting to others? Do you make up stories about why someone said something or did you imagine someone whispering about you? Are you just like Lucy–caught in your show?

When you can pull yourself back to be the observer–just like you are when you sit in the audience watching a show–you put yourself in a power position to see the Truth clearly. The Truth may not always look like what you want, but it is a safe place to make decisions.

Be aware that being in the observer state is not a state of fully being or fully living. It is an observational state that can give you a quick hit of clarity before you scream at Ricky! Those who get stuck in the observational state are about a step up from the ditch. Remember, it is a place to gain perspective so you can return to your life.

True You Tool

The Drama-free Zone: Practice Being the Observer

The next time you are in a passionate conversation with a friend or a relative, instead of reacting to the words, give yourself space between the words and the point of these words. Connect with your body and be present. Say to yourself, "I now see clearly." When you are actively and consciously engaged in drama, you are Lucy. When you pull back and disconnect from the current information, you are the viewer at home. There's no emotion, there's no investment, there's just feedback from what you are observing. This is just a slight difference, and yet it makes all the difference in the world when it comes to avoiding drama.

If you've ever been in an argument you wanted to win, where you wanted to convince someone else to believe what you believe, then you've experienced the pull of the drama. When you are not attached to outcomes, it's easier to disengage and move to observing what is going on for you and for the other person. Suddenly, you can see the other person's motivations. You can feel what is pulling at you. From this disengaged place, you can decide–*consciously choose*–what to do.

What is the feedback telling you? What do you need to do more or less of? How can you pull the Truth out and leave the story behind?

You can practice this at home very easily. As you watch TV, don't get emotionally engaged. Just watch the performers. Don't think of them as the character, think of them as people, and see the edges of the TV, open up to observing the actors acting. Practice going back and forth so you can be in the show and outside of it. Once you get the hang of this technique, you will always have it. This is a great place to go when you feel your emotions taking over.

Note your experiences here:

Of the many tools I have, this is one that can create a peaceful calm in your life that many people never know exists. Drama is not a requirement of living big and creating your dreams.

Section III

Claiming The Winning Ticket, a.k.a. Surprise! YOU Are The Golden Ticket!

"You might not believe it's possible to create your life in your own way. However, if you've spent any time at all creating your life by everyone else's way, you know deep inside of yourself that there must be an easier way. There is. Yours! Your life's path will be uniquely yours, will feel good and will be easier because it is yours to create any way you like."

-Tina Ferguson

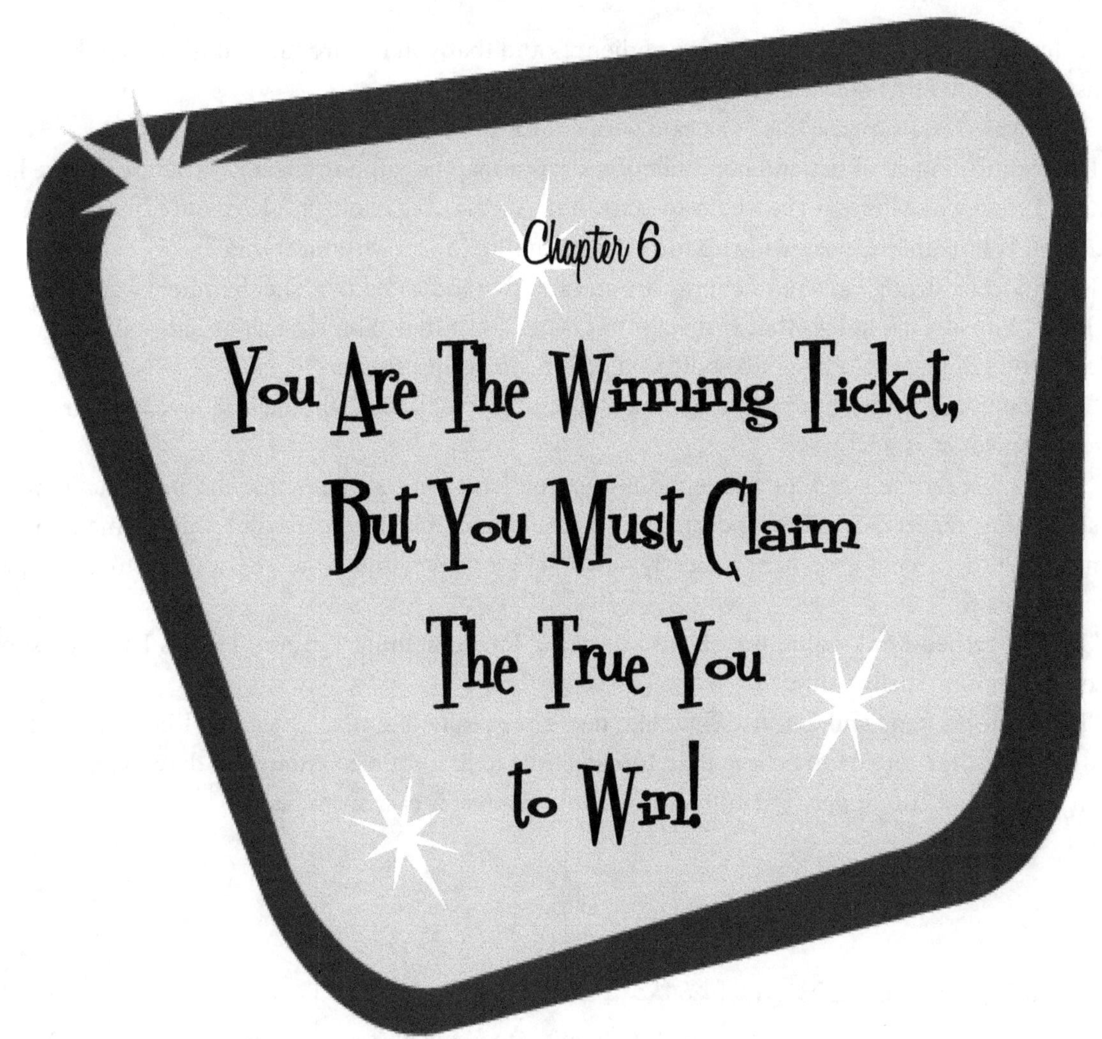

"If you ask me what I came into this life to do, I will tell you:
I came to live out loud."
-Emile Zola

"I see a woman that looks like Sally Field in a red dress walking on a stage," I said. "Are you a speaker?" In my mind's vision, I could see a petite, brunette woman walking on a large stage and I could feel a tremendous amount of energy and enthusiasm underneath the image I had in mind. It didn't occur to me to ask if the woman on the phone, Shelly, was an actor. She felt like a dynamo speaker to me.

"Yes, I am," Shelly answered. "But I'm not the kind of speaker I want to be yet," she added hastily.

"It feels like you want to reach bigger audiences and that you inspire these audiences to believe in themselves. Would that be true?" I asked.

"Well, yes. Yes, I suppose it is," she said with enthusiasm.

Between the image of her and her audience, I saw a map hanging in the air. "You aren't sure how to make it happen–where to go, where to start, but don't worry about it," I reassured her. "You are *already* on your path. Keep showing up for what is coming to you without trying."

I could feel a strong current of energy around her that indicated that she definitely was already in the flow. "You already know what you want to create. Trust that. You have your entire life to go and settle for something else. Why not be bold and go for something greater?"

"You don't know this, but people tell me all the time I look like Sally Field. I love to wear red on stage. It's one of my signatures."

"Well, I can certainly feel the tremendous love you have for your audience and that you are ready for something bigger," I said wondering what could possibly have brought this woman to this moment in time. I could see her so clearly, and the energy around what she wanted to create was powerfully swift.

"I'm concerned I'm kidding myself into thinking I'm something I'm not. I guess I wanted some sort of validation," Shelly confided.

"I see you on stage and I hear, 'They like me. They really like me,'" I said as I described what I could see. "It's time for you to believe that, too. It's time to like yourself enough to dare to put yourself out on stage–front and center. They *already* like you–the rest is easy from here."

Notice the True You–Do you like the True You?

Are you like Shelly? Looking for outside validation to *know* it's safe to come out and play? Do you question what you *already* know is true–what is *True You*? As you sit reading this book, be aware that there is the reader and there is the *True You*. The reader is going to read the book, take in the bits of information, announce various declarations about what he or she thinks and believes and pass on direction–or not–to *you*.

The *True You* is just underneath the reader. It's the part of you that feels pulled to get up and go for a walk, to let this information soak into you.

Shelly knew she was talented. She was a top-notch executive in a large company, and though she routinely presented sales proposals, her heart's work was about showing up in a much grander fashion–and on a much bigger stage. Her desire felt soulful, not driven by an external need or other lower motivation.

The cautious, thinking part of her wanted to be sure of success *before* she committed to her soul's path and took an action. In the land of *True You*, you take inspired action, and as you do, you feel even *surer.* The mind will never have enough evidence to feel completely safe and protected, although some evidence (such as an example of someone who is doing what you want to do) can enable you to let go of the need for ultimate control.

When you step into your *True You,* you will easily move away from trying to make things happen and trying to plan and gather evidence for what you already know is true. Your *True You* is the fiber optic line that is hooked up to the part of you that was born ready. Your soul already knows all you are capable of being.

Follow these subtle nudges that are asking you to plug back into your life. Act on them as you work this program. Let your heart out of prison and see what it has to share with you. You just might be surprised with what you find.

Identifying What You Really Want

What do you really want from this book? Why are you reading it? Be honest. What are you searching for? It may come out as something you don't want, or it may come out as something you do want. List your answers here. If your answers come in the form of don't wants, turn those into do wants:

I Don't Want My Life to Be…	I Do Want My Life to Be…

Take a good look at your answers to be sure what you've written is the Truth. Be sure, too, that it is *your* Truth. This is *your* life, and *you* are the only one who can live it. Remember, you've committed to changing your life and to discovering the *True You.* It's just you, God and the legion of heavenly messengers with you right now. Claim your ticket!

People want to win the lottery so they can live their dream life, but when you live your life in the present each day, your life becomes the lottery. Marie, a dear friend, said this to me one day. How true!

One day, I'll…When I get to this weight, then I'll…When I get married, then…

Each moment you have is like a gold coin given to you by the Creator. If you were required to give a gold coin for every second you are alive, you would soon see how your life *does* resemble the lottery. Your life is given freely, without strings, for you to spend any way you like. How will you spend your precious treasure?

There is no 'one day'–this is it. Living is a verb, not a noun. That means it is marked by action. Being is an intentional state, so even 'being' requires action.

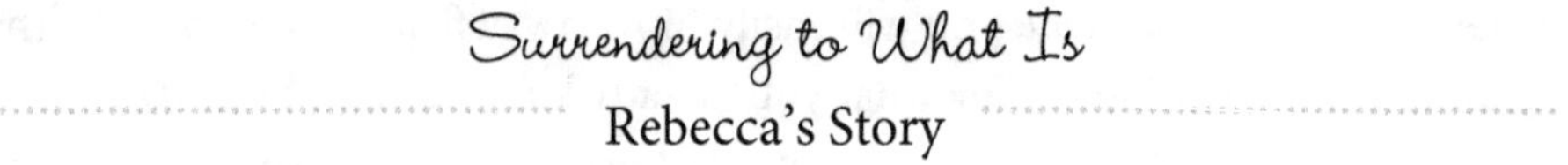

Surrendering to What Is

Rebecca's Story

Rebecca was a smart, funny woman with a high-powered job, a fabulous fiancé and everything a young professional could ask for–and then some. Fifty pounds overweight, the baggage she held about being overweight overshadowed nearly everything in her life. Time and time again, she commented on the extra pounds she carried around her torso like a barrel. And now, to top it off, "My fiancé wants to go to the beach for vacation!" she exclaimed.

"You have two choices," I pointed out. You can either lose weight, or you can love yourself just as you are and live with it. If you don't, you are going to miss all the living available to you now because your focus is on all of these pounds you want to disown. Do you want memories or do you want to spend more time focusing on what's not working?"

I didn't hear her talk about the subject again until about a year later when she called. "I want to thank you for bringing my attention to what I was doing with my obsessiveness with my weight. I realized I was making myself and everyone else crazy with my discontent. After that, I went to the beach, got over myself and had a great time. Since I made peace with myself, I've lost 30 pounds. Can you believe it?"

I loved hearing her news. Not only did she start focusing on what was important–really important to her–she accepted the area of herself that once held the energy of self-hatred, which then allowed that area to lovingly melt away.

Right Here, Right Now

What Holds Your *True You* Back

Identify all the things that hold you back from acting in this moment. Include people you resent, secrets that haunt you, unforgiveness that holds you prisoner, fears that bind and any other belief that comes between you and your dreams:

* ______
* ______
* ______
* ______

* ____________________
* ____________________
* ____________________
* ____________________
* ____________________
* ____________________

Use a notebook and make a page for each of the areas above, if you want. Put people on one page, secrets on another, for example. For most people, this process can take months of dedicated effort to 'clear' the air and make peace with the past. Use the Power of Forgiveness Meditation (page 57) to reset and neutralize the energy for each area. Don't forget to include yourself! Now, take a look at your list and ask yourself which areas need more of your loving attention.

What actions will you take on these areas? By when?

* ____________________

  Date____________
* ____________________

  Date____________
* ____________________

  Date____________

Love is Not a Four-Letter Word on a Greeting Card

The basis of this program is love. Unconditional, unapologetic, strong, supportive love that can move *anything*. When you love yourself no matter what, you will not be looking for a designer label to tell you that you belong and that you are good. You will not be looking for another person to 'complete' you. Your next achievement will not 'make' or 'break' you.

You will understand that you are every ingredient of the cupcake that is your life. From the wrapper that holds you, to the perfect mix of ingredients, to the creamy, sweet frosting. You are already every part of what you want to be, and when others join you, it is a cupcake celebration where the party gets bigger, not where you have to take parts of you away to get the love you need.

Practice Outrageous Love

Love is the strongest force on the planet. You have within you the strongest, most protective energy that will keep you safe, comfort you and at all times assist you in living. This love is always present, always available.

I believe the greatest pain we will ever feel in this world results from the illusion that we are separate from what we are-love. It is such an alluring idea to the person in pain, and it is not even real! When we feel alone (remember Heart Flash #13: You are never, ever alone), we make up all kinds of stories that create a big cage that imprisons our heart. "He doesn't care about me…" "How can I do this alone?…" "No one would even care if I wasn't here anymore…" All lies disconnect us from ourselves and from God.

If you think about it, we *can't* be alone. From the moment you open your eyes in the morning, others are connected to you. The people who ensure the electricity works, who manage the clean water coming out of the tap, those who keep the stoplights working, the trash pick-up that works like clockwork…we are indelibly connected to others. When you practice gratitude for all the unknown people who enable your life to flow, you will experience outrageous love. You will see that you are also part of others' lives in a way you probably never considered. Soon you will feel sweeping joy for the riches in your life.

Connection is what life is all about. Without it, what is the point of living? Your connection is as guaranteed as gravity. It's always there waiting for you. Ultimately, this connection is love.

To practice outrageous love, begin acting as if you are in love with everyone on the planet. When you look in the mirror, look at yourself and feel that you love that person looking back at you more than anything else in the world. Don't overcomplicate the process. Don't think about it. *Just do it*, as Nike says.

Let the garbage, the junk, the judgments, the critical ideas float to the surface and float away. Then look at yourself again and say, "I love you." Throw in a few other compliments, and you are on your way to a great day. Remember, you have two choices–Past Perfect Turnpike and Fast Forward Turnpike. Fast Forward is about moving forward and allowing the junk to be pushed out by the *True You*. As you show up in *you*, then the other things shift and move away from you. You can use the tools in this book to make peace and forgive, and you can simply see the Truth and let the false slide away.

If you spend time wanting to know *why* you feel this way, it will take that much longer because *why* is the entry point for the land of distractions and detours. Why not do something different this time?

When you meet people on the street, love them, too. They are doing the best they can–just like you are. Give them the benefit of the doubt. Choose to see the best in them. Disarm them with love if they are unkind. The more love you send out, the more love comes back to you. Fall in love with yourself and the world again in a big, big way!

Your nature is to be loving. When you were born, you loved everyone and everything. You didn't know about protecting your fragile ego. You accepted people and loved fully. If you don't feel loving, it's likely you are out of practice. Or, perhaps, it is because you don't feel loved yourself. If you have just committed to love yourself no matter what, that won't be a challenge for very long.

Crystal Clear Clarity

Oh, How You Can Love Yourself!

Name three things (or more) you LOVE about yourself:

1. ______________________________
2. ______________________________
3. ______________________________

Now, think about someone, something or some experience you *love*. Bring that feeling up in your body and hold it. Notice how it feels peaceful and safe. Take it in and feel it in every part of your body. This is the love *you* have inside of you *for you*. Hold that love and think of yourself–think of these three things and then immerse your whole body in this feeling. Bathe yourself in this love–the love the *True You* has to share with you.

Anytime you are feeling that others do not like you, do not understand you, are judging you or anything else that is external and outside of you, go back to this feeling and love yourself. Give yourself what you want from others and soon you will have that love from them, too.

You Are in Charge–Despite Current Beliefs!

For the next two days, I want you relentlessly to monitor your thoughts. Don't judge them–just monitor what is going in and out of your mind. We are looking for the thoughts that are creating your current experience. There's no right or wrong. These are what they are. Your current experience is a continuous feedback loop for what your focus is; however, this type of monitoring will supercharge your awareness. You will be able to claim your life in a way that will show you, without a doubt, that you are calling to you many experiences all the time. Before long, your mind will actually believe that you just might be part of the process, and the thoughts swirling around are powerful.

These thoughts may be contrary to the life you *want* to live and to the Truth that you are. The goal is to catch these thoughts and then release them by replacing the thought with a thought that matches your Truth. It takes very little of this conscious choice to make a big difference. Do not wait for this–there's no time like the present. Even five minutes can offer you extraordinary benefits.

Right Here, Right Now

Your Thoughts

Grab the closest piece of paper to do this next exercise.

Create a table like the one below or go to http://www.TinaFerguson.com/mbp for another form. Use this form to catch the thoughts that are supportive, that find you being *True You.* Are there any other thoughts trailing behind that are not supporting you? Notice any and all thoughts. There are no 'bad' thoughts–they are just what you are thinking at that moment. When you feel emotional, pay special attention to the thoughts that arise. When you feel others are against you...When you are overwhelmed...When things don't go as you planned. Is this reflective of your life? Record them. Don't think too much, just allow them to flow. If you notice a lot of thoughts that leave you feeling down, use the Connect to Love tool on page 11 or use the emergency toolkit on page 199.

This is a critical step in increasing your awareness of your inner space. If you feel that this is too much work, then do it for *one minute at a time.* Even five or 10 minutes can be beneficial. The more overwhelmed you feel, the more this can help you. As you practice and spend more time in the 'present,' you'll be able to notice these thoughts more easily. Start where you are and do your best. Commit as little as five or 10 minutes to this exercise. An hour can dramatically shift your life.

Time & How I Felt	My Thought	What Happened Before	What I Told Myself
Ex: 7 *AM/Worried*	Ex: *I can't do this.*	Ex: *Thought about problem.*	Ex: *I always have problems.*

"You want me to do what?" she asked incredulously. "I can't keep track of all of my thoughts. They are racing one on top of each other. You've got to be kidding!"

Jessica, a sensitive, smart woman in her 50s who had faced a sudden breakup, began working with me to, as she put it, "find herself." After a sudden split with her husband of five years, she felt abandoned, unplugged, exhausted and fried. The pain of the separation was nothing compared to the thoughts she was suffocating under.

"I know it sounds like a lot of work. Your thinking mind may not know how to do something new that might make it easier for you to be in charge for a change," I said. "But you are in charge of your mind. If you will trust me and do this for only a day-I know that it will significantly reduce what seems overwhelming."

"When I work with people, the energy in their mind looks like tornadoes swirling in their head," I explained. "People think they are thinking or figuring out a problem, but what they are doing is running around the track in their mind over and over again. This circular thinking begins to lift, and soon it is like you have a tornado running through your mind."

"That's exactly how I feel," she answered. "Now how do I do this so I can get this to stop?"

I gave Jessica the instructions that I am giving you here. These are the steps to redirect the mental thinking motor mind and get back on track. People with the most desperate cases can clear this energy and get back on track within a week, and so can you. Clearing space inside is critical to claiming your ticket.

What You Are and What You Are Not

Let's start with what you are not. You are not:

- Your job.
- Your job title.
- Your quota.
- Your weight.
- Your designer label.
- Your designer purse, suit, shoes.
- Your luxury car.
- Your bank account.
- Your promotion.
- Your marital status.
- Your religion.
- Your beliefs.

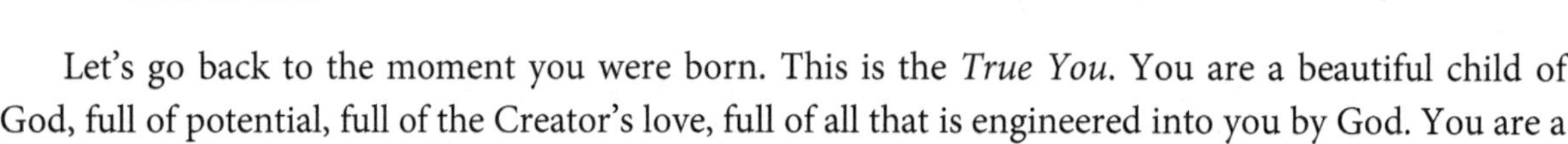

Let's go back to the moment you were born. This is the *True You.* You are a beautiful child of God, full of potential, full of the Creator's love, full of all that is engineered into you by God. You are a natural creator!

Back then, you had no idea about what a designer label was, you had no clue that you or perhaps your parents weren't 'cool,' you couldn't have cared less about your weight and you definitely weren't concerned about a job, marital status or your religion.

You were perfectly imperfect. Completely accepted for who you were. Utterly content with what you had. Sure that what you didn't have would be provided for you. All you had to do was ask. You did this in many ways, quite naturally, and life began.

Somewhere between that time and now, lots of things happened, some labeled 'good,' some labeled 'bad.' The bad ones were sorted into a pile of "don't do that again," and the good ones filed in your mind under "these get me what I want." The more you play with the good, the more you get what you want, and the more you do the bad, the more you pay the price and get punished.

It all seems so *simple.* Except that it's not true. However, you don't know that. You don't realize that because you are still operating like you are a child and under the influences of all of the labels you filed away while growing up. Today, we are claiming your winning ticket–you!

? True You Question

Who are you?

Let's go back to the time when you really did know who you are. You are probably about five or six. You've learned some of the game rules, but you are still enough of who you really are to remember what you like, what you don't like, to know that you have an opinion, and to be able to express what you want to be when you grow up. Can you remember what that was?

Moving forward, from age seven to 12, your mind is developing and you are taking notice of your natural talents. These talents grab your attention. If you are particularly good at sports, maybe you spend lots of time in sports, or maybe you are a dancer and you spend hours practicing tap and ballet. Are you an artist? What did you want to be when you were this age?

Finally, you are moving into the most intense part of the game of life. We begin to learn about acceptance by peers and those outside of our family. From age 13 to 21, what is on your mind? How have you changed how you feel about yourself? What do you feel about others? Where are your dreams now? What did you want to be at this age?

I wanted to be Wonder Woman for as long as I could remember. I had a pencil box that had Snoopy on it and I would put my pencils and erasers in it. I would hold it up and pretend it was my magic bracelet, shielding me from the words coming from others. I can't remember what I wanted to be specifically at age six, but I knew I wanted to be a beautiful woman who was powerful–just like Wonder Woman.♥

–Kristine, age 32

Today, who are you? What mix of words do you use to describe yourself? Words help us define our focus. What do you notice about your focus?

* Is it on the things you do or a label of who you are? *"I am a CEO," "I am a mother," "I am an entrepreneur," "I am a teacher," "I am an attorney."*
* Is it focused on results? *"I am a successful business owner," "I am a best-selling author," "I am a multi-millionaire."*
* Is it on what you have? *"I am a Lexus owner," "I am a home owner."*
* Is it on your beliefs? *"I am a conservationist," "I am a Republican or Democrat." "I am an activist," "I am a philanthropist," "I am Catholic."*
* Is it on how you are feeling? *"I am lonely," "I am angry," "I am frustrated," "I am happy," "I am grateful," "I am passionate."*
* Is it on what you value? *"I am kind," "I am integrity," "I am love," "I am peace," "I am aware," "I am..."*

Using the Connect to Love tool, on page 11, immerse yourself in the feeling of love. Now, talk to the *True You*–your inner self. What do you want to tell yourself about who you know you are?

I am. . .

I am really great because. . .

I am best when. . .

Say Goodbye to The Victim Mindset!

When you are ready to unite with your Truth, the tools for change find you. Discovering the *True You* is one of the most rewarding forms of change you will find. It is well worth the effort–*you are well worth the effort!*

By now, you have started to accept and love yourself unconditionally. You have taken responsibility for your thoughts. You have made a claim on who you really are and are claiming your ticket to living fully, creatively and decisively!

There's one more stop. It's time to take off the mask of the victim and put it right where it belongs–in the garbage!

Many years ago, a wise friend once said to me, "No one cares, Tina. Get over yourself." It was like being dowsed with a frigid glass of water. I blinked my eyes almost in disbelief of the words, and then I began to consider them.

My friend's comment came from my concern about something someone had said about me that wasn't true. I couldn't believe I would be part of gossip, and it threw me into this concern about others thinking about me in a way I did not like. The Truth was I *knew* it wasn't true. Did I care other people maybe thought it was true? Yes, I did. Could I change it? Yes, I could. Was it worth making a fuss about it? No, it wasn't. I saw the truth in what she was saying. People have a 'topic' of the week–some even have a topic of the day. Gossiping about someone else's life, woes or issues is a great distraction from looking at–and living–your own life. When that happened, it wasn't about me; it was about them–it's about them needing to put other people down so they could, at least for a time, feel better about themselves. That's what my friend was trying to say. Whether the topic of the week is you, or Britney Spears, or Paris Hilton, or a host of others, none of it matters unless *you* decide it matters.

In every situation, you have three choices: Accept it, change it or let it go. *You choose.* By knowing that you *always* have a choice, you never, ever have to be a victim again.

I see people struggle with their choices. They struggle with their power. They agonize over which choice to make. Many people think a right way and a wrong way exist. This is unfortunate because thinking like this introduces fear into every agonizing decision. When you work with the Heart Flashes and realize that every moment is reaching out to you from Truth, you can connect to yourself and make a decision from Truth. If you don't like it later, you simply create something new. There's no fear here–it's just you.

Again, the Fast Forward Turnpike says transform through action in your *True You* beingness *as you live your life out loud.* Try out your new tools, knowing you can always get the love you need from yourself. Some people may *not* like it when you work with your power. But, the only way this person is in your world is if some part of you is afraid of your power. It's not them–it's you. So what? Peer into yourself and ask, '*What am I afraid of?*'–you'll find your answers there.

If you are afraid of losing people, I can assure you that this is a common concern. This also can be another distraction–another reason to put off being all that you *already* are. Those who love you–*truly* love you–will get over themselves enough to celebrate with you. And, those who don't, well, they will have your life to illuminate theirs as they learn more about themselves.

You are not responsible for how other people feel. When you come from a place of love for yourself and when you are kind and loving to others, you will soon see that there are many other people out there who will love to be in your presence–in your present.

You will hear me say this often. You will not know the Truth until you try it. You can remain on Struggle Street, or you can claim your lottery ticket and move to Easy Street. Your choice–*always.*

Crystal Clear Clarity

Say Good-bye to The Victim Mindset

Areas, people, situations where I don't feel like I have a choice are:

I stay in these situations or with these people because I believe I am getting:

Be honest. It's just you, your heavenly messengers and me here! I've never liked the word victim. It sounds so, well, *helpless*. But isn't that what a victim is? I believe that we inherit the victim mindset. However, we don't have to continue working with it once we see we have a *choice* to move to empowerment.

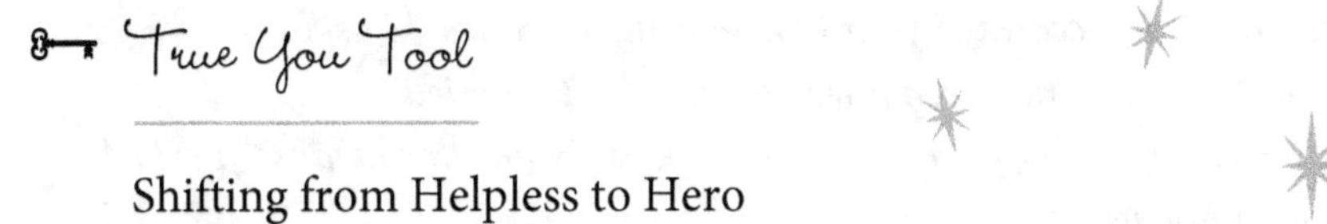

Shifting from Helpless to Hero

The fastest way to move from helpless to hero is to flip from victim mindset into creator mindset. If you find yourself thinking… "I can't…How do I?…" then flip into your creator mindset and ask, "What do I *choose* to create right now? What do I choose to *feel* right now? What *can* I do right now?" Take just one step and be prepared for the next steps to appear for you. This is a powerful tool. If you like, Connect to Love first (page 11) and then work from there.

What do you need right now?

We all have needs. Some needs are 'would be nice to have' wants and other needs are 'non-negotiable.' Do you know what your needs are? A good place to begin is back at the previous *Crystal Clear Clarity*. Your non-negotiable needs are those things you need so you can be yourself. There is no room for negotiation–period. Claim your needs!

Claiming Your True You Needs

Paula's Story

Paula was a chipper, spunky 50-something executive who called asking for a session right away. I knew other people who knew her, but we had never personally met each other. We set an appointment for a few days later.

I learned that she had a huge burden hanging over her head and needed to be in the space of non-judgment. She needed to be herself without fear. Soon it was apparent that she was living a lie in her own home. Her husband was a meticulous, neat person who did not like clutter and who did not care much for holidays. She, on the other hand, prized possessions and loved to decorate to the nines for the holidays.

"Paula, when was the last time you decorated your home for the holidays?" I asked.

A loud sigh came across the phone. "It has been a while–since I got married."

"I see Halloween decorations hanging on your door–do you know what this means?" I asked as I shared the visions flashing in my head.

"I love to decorate for Halloween and give out candy. I usually dress up, too. I really love it; it's one of my favorite holidays," she gushed with bubbly energy.

I replied, "Then you must do this–there has to be some way you and your husband can honor each other while you have your needs met, too. I want you to promise me that you will decorate this year." I felt like this was an urgent message to return to her Truth and challenged her dismissive demeanor.

I could hear the hesitation in her voice. "Paula," I said. "This is not something you can just amputate out of you. This is a reflection of who you are. How can it work? I know you can find a way for this to work. When you express yourself fully, your husband is the recipient of the creativity you exude. This isn't just for you; it's for both of you. Honor what your soul needs to express. There is always time and space for who you are in God's world."

Unfortunately, this story doesn't have a happy ending. Paula passed away just a couple of years later. I cried as I listened to the eulogy that brought these visions back to me and reminded me that we all have a chance to choose life each and every moment. Let Paula be your cheerleader to express yourself and dare to live out loud.

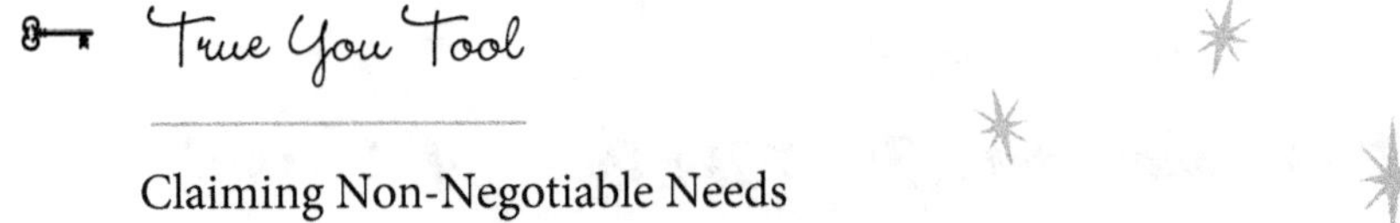

Claiming Non-Negotiable Needs

Your needs *do* matter. When you honor yourself, you have more to give. You are not being selfish; you are actually being more loving when you give to yourself first. When we are present for ourselves, we share our entire being with those around us. You won't have the strength to support others pulling themselves out of the ditch if you don't take care of yourself. Needs are not wants. Wants are things you desire that you don't currently have but that you can live without–a new car, a larger house, a pool. Non-negotiable needs are different in that they are related to your well-being and the very fabric of who you are.

Things I Want	Things I Need to Be My True Self (Non-negotiable Needs)
Ex: *A housekeeper.*	Ex: *Time alone in nature.*

Non-negotiable needs change you when they are not met. This is why they are non-negotiable when you honor the *True You*. Often, what you need is what stands between you, what you want and how you most want to express yourself.

A Personal Story From The Queen of Dreams

When Chance, our son, was a baby, like many new parents I didn't get much uninterrupted sleep. As an intuitive, sleep is extremely important to my well-being. The more I tried to work without sleep, the worse I felt. The more I tried to be stoic, to show I could get along with little sleep, the more I became this person I didn't even want to be around!

Finally, I realized that if I wanted to be the best mom and wife I could be, I had to find some way to get sleep. How did I do this? It was as easy as asking. I talked to my husband about what I really needed to be more 'me.' He was missing my bubbly fun presence, so he was eager to help. Within an hour, we put a plan in place that would deliver both of us what we most desired, which was really more of 'me.' Our life magically changed for the better practically overnight. I remember this anytime I'm putting off taking care of myself because I realize my well-being is not just for me; it's for my entire family.♥

As simple as that sounds, this is a good example of how we deny ourselves even the most basic things we require to be who we are. When you honor, nurture and care for yourself, you will always be cared for. Claim your golden ticket!

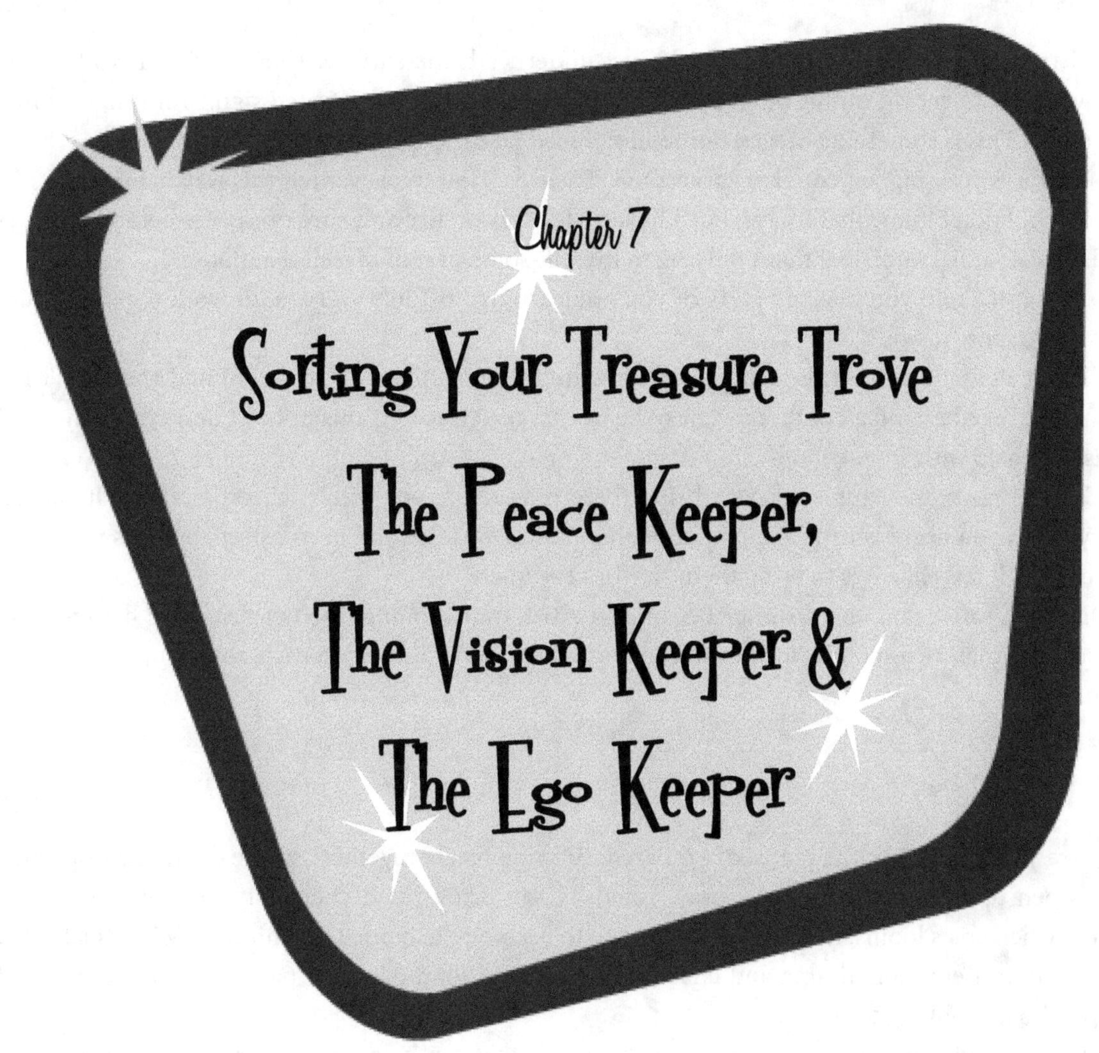

Chapter 7
Sorting Your Treasure Trove The Peace Keeper, The Vision Keeper & The Ego Keeper

"Ordinary riches can be stolen, real riches cannot. In your soul are infinitely precious things that cannot be taken from you."

–Oscar Wilde

"It feels like I have more going on inside of me than just me," she said. "There's a part of me that is excited. I can feel that I'm moving in a new direction and it just feels *right.* But, then there's this other part of me that is demanding my attention. I swear it's like I'm in between parts of myself."

"Which one do you trust?" I asked the successful attorney on the phone. I recognized in her the contrast I had seen in other clients who were switching from leading with their minds to leading with their hearts.

"I trust the excited part; it feels *right* just underneath the surface. I guess what I really want to know is how to get rid of this other piece of me," she said with a frustrated sigh. "I mean, I know I'm not crazy. This is something bigger. Something I haven't experienced before. I know it."

"What is your biggest concern about this?" I asked. "Have you ever felt this way before?"

"Nah, I don't know that I have, but I haven't felt this on fire and sure of my life before either," she said. "I guess I'm concerned that I'm lying to myself–some part of myself, I suppose."

"What if I told you that the parts of you are learning, just like you are, to work together? Would that make sense to you?"

"That's exactly what it feels like–like there are these members of my team and they don't know how to be together and all of them want to be in charge at once. At this point, I don't even know what to ask for help with."

"There are some simple ways to bring these into alignment with each other, Tara. It can seem scary when you begin getting acquainted with a part of you that has been asleep, but it is really much easier than it feels like it is to teach them to work together."

Not long after that, this attorney became an artist, transitioning into her heart and her life's work. It took less than two months for her to integrate the parts of herself so each could support her soul's path.

Are you feeling like the pieces of you aren't playing nicely together? In the ditch, the opportunity is to open up to yourself in a new way. Intensity can bring rapid change–if you will work with it. Often, when crisis looms, the heart has a chance to become the hero. The Thinking Mind is left almost useless amidst emotion, drama and chaos. The heart can illuminate the path out of the darkness for those who are looking for it.

Understand that you have different pieces of you that can help you sort the treasure trove so you can pinpoint what part is talking and wants your attention. Realizing that there are many pieces of you can help you shine brightly and know which part of you is seeking balance.

The Thinking Mind, a.k.a. The Ego Keeper

The Thinking Mind is the conscious part of you, the part of you that you are aware of. It may speak to you in thought forms and ideas. If your thinking mind is super active, it may talk to you in a running commentary. It is the part of you that has direct conversations in your mind and which may look at the pros and cons of a situation. It may have thoughts about others while you are in the middle of conversation… "Who does she think she is?" or "What do I say to her to get her to stop?"

The Thinking Mind is self-directed, which means you are directing it. This is important. People often feel like they do not get to choose what they think. When the thoughts are coming fast and furious from many different points, you may feel as if you don't get a choice at all. Rest assured that you do!

The thinking mind is concerned with rules and structure. What do we need to do? When do we need to do it? What is important to achieving our goal? This part of you is in charge, to varying degrees, of keeping things under control. It is the 'grown-up' side of you that says, "Hold in the tears" when you've been reprimanded by your boss. It's also the part of you that says, "Let's go. We have things to do."

Many people think the Thinking Mind is who they are. They have identified with this part of themselves for so long, they actually can begin to believe they are their obsessions, compulsions and thinking. Nothing could be farther from the truth. The more you link to your heart, the more the *True You* will shine through. Make no doubt, though, that the Thinking Mind is a wonderful servant for your heart. When you feel *good*, your heart and Thinking Mind are in harmony. Your feelings guide you toward the Truth. If your Thinking Mind is too busy, then you can slip into the Motor Mind.

The Motor Mind

Because you have never been given an owner's manual for your inner being and likely have no idea that you–the *True You*–is really in charge, you might be surprised to find out that you call the shots. The Thinking Mind is a workhorse. It is a steady servant that will do any job you ask it to do. The problem is your mind probably hasn't been given a *real* job in a very long time. Without a job, or a focus, the Thinking Mind runs laps around the track chasing whatever it is you are focusing on in the moment. That is when the Motor Mind can put you on a lap (or two, or 10, or 20) around the track.

If your mind doesn't have something to occupy it (and that can be stillness even though stillness seems like nothing, it actually is a lot). Without some type of focus, your mind will become restless and naturally find something to do. If you have ever seen a racecar going around a track over and over again, then you have an idea of what you are energetically doing in your mind as you retrace thoughts repeatedly. Often, you may even feel that you are just a spectator in your show, that you don't get to choose your thoughts–the thoughts are coming and coming and you are just along for the ride. A mind without a job becomes the Motor Mind taking laps around the track. This can leave you feeling exhausted and tired–both in your head and in your life.

Without a destination, the workhorse Thinking Mind has nowhere to go, nothing to do. It is designed to focus and go. Without a higher focus, the focus becomes whatever the last attention point was. That could be the insult you felt in the elevator as a woman looked you up and down with a hint of judgment in her eyes. Or, it might be the argument you had with your lover last night. Soon the Motor Mind is making laps around the track, "What's wrong with how I'm dressed? I look fine." "I'm so tired of people treating me like that." Or, "What is going on with people these days?" Or in the case of the argument, "I can see his point, but he needs to see mine, too." "I really don't care what he thinks, my point is important." On and on, the motor mind runs around the track, making no ground and getting nowhere.

When you take a look at your life, you may find that this is how your day is every single day. It begins with rehashing what happened the night before until *Ping!* you run into a new diversion to rehash and then *Whammo!* there's another one for the Motor Mind to chase. Where are *you* in all of this? Do you have visions of a car running around the track with you being dragged behind it? I hope so–that's exactly what you are experiencing!

You may *think* this is you. It is not. This is your Motor Mind's mess. This is *not* you. You are not the collection of thoughts streaming through your head. You are not the political debate you had last night. You are not the job title you see when you enter your office. This is the ego's domain. This is what many people *associate* with as themselves, but this is just the show for now.

Think back to Lucy TV–Lucy is Lucy until she is caught up in the drama. Then you can almost see the Motor Mind take root and off she goes, scheming, trying to fix things, and moving things around. Her Motor Mind is off to the races, lap after lap after lap. How close is this to your own experience? Jot your thoughts here:

____

____

____

____

____

____

____

____

____

____

True You Tool

The Motor Mind

Your Motor Mind plays an important role, so give it a name. The point of this program is not to disown *any* part of who you are. It works to get all the parts of you working together for your greater good. Name your Motor Mind: ______________________________

Think about the last time you worked with your Motor mind. When was the last time you went around the track and wanted to stop, but ______________________________, a.k.a. Motor Mind, wouldn't 'let' you. Bring that feeling and state of being up in your body right now. Hint: Just the memory will evoke it for you.

Now, with this feeling coursing through your body, take a deep breath and ask the following questions:

- What part of this thought needs my attention? What part of me needs my attention?
- How do I feel right now? (Note where you feel tense or anxious.)
- How do I want to feel right now?
- What do I want to feel what I want right now?

This is similar to shining the light of Truth. It gets the Motor Mind off your back and by asking, "What do I want to feel right now?" gives your Thinking Mind a job to do.

When you begin to notice the different parts of you, it can be a magical experience. Suddenly, you feel more empowered, more in control of what you are thinking, feeling and doing. Soon, you begin to notice the *True You* making more appearances throughout the day and you say things and think, "Where did *that* come from?"

The Motor Mind is important because it helps to tip you off that your Thinking Mind needs a job and that you are perhaps 'checked out.' Remember, all parts of you combine to work with you. The Ego Keeper brings in new experiences, new ideas and lessons that urge you to reunite with the Truth inside. In this way, it is a benevolent ruler (though it might not feel like that) that will rule until you decide to consciously rule for yourself.

Too many people have tried to disown the mind–the constant state of irritation and thought forms they don't like. Life is much easier if you make peace with all the parts of you and *work together*. Carl Jung, the great psychologist said, "What you resist, persists." Don't resist this part of yourself–it is bringing you closer to the *True You.*

In Tara's example, her Thinking Mind was always in charge and always followed 'the rules' she learned as a young child. The rules were marching around in her head: 'Be responsible,' 'Don't throw away your life on a dream,' 'You've worked hard to get here, don't throw it away.' All these rules were floating to the top as she embarked on her real dream of being an artist. Her inner struggle was not with anyone else but with the programming she was carrying around in her subconscious–*programming she wasn't even aware she had.* Soon she was able to discern the Motor Mind from the Thinking Mind, which then worked tirelessly to support her soul's desire.

Working With the Thinking Mind

The Thinking Mind–the conscious focus of your attention right now–is the part of you that is responsible for holding the Vision Point. Let's say that you want to get out of the crisis you are in. Your Thinking Mind's 'job' is to hold the Vision Point. The Vision Point is always changing. So today the Vision Point might be to feel calm amidst the chaos. Tomorrow the Vision Point might be to get a job. The next day the Vision Point might be to be outside in the sunshine. Moment to moment, the Vision Point changes with your focus.

The Thinking Mind is powerful, but it is only as powerful as its Vision Point. A powerful Vision Point like this is akin to a big Clydesdale horse with blinder's on that can do a lot of work for you and can get you up a hill, over the mountain and through the valley. If the vision is strong enough, it can stay the course through virtually any emotional water you come across.

Remember that the Thinking Mind works best with a specific, direct Vision Point. A series of these Vision Points along a path may look like mini destination points. For example, let's say you are getting a divorce and feel horrible about it. Your vision points might look like this:

- Day 1 – Determine what I truly want to create and how I want the divorce to play out.
- Day 2 – Determine what I need right now and give it to myself.
- Day 3 – Make a list of things we need to do to work together.
- Day 4 – Determine from the list what I can do by myself.
- Day 5 – Create my best case scenario schedule.
- Day 6 – Look for a new home.

Each day, your mind has a Vision Point. Your ultimate Vision Point might be to be in another relationship that is loving and compassionate, but that vision happens as a result of taking care of the here and now. You can make moment-to-moment Vision Points if you are in the depths of despair (see page 199 for steps). Sometimes when you are in the darkness, just working moment to moment is the safest place to be. Thinking about tomorrow is too far off. At other times, you might look hour to hour, or half-day to half-day; work with whatever works best for you.

Moment to moment, if you do not know a specific action, then your Vision Point can be to simply *feel* what you most want to feel. Joy...calm...peace...love...play with different Vision Points to see what works best for you.

True You Tool

Creating an Intention

Think of something you want to do or accomplish that you have not done. One thing will usually come easily to mind because you have been frustrated that you haven't taken action on it.

I will:

By (date):

I don't know how; that doesn't matter. I know what I do know. Write the first things that pop into your mind. You may only get one or two, usually not more than three at a time if you stay in your heart. If it helps, Connect to Love (page 11) first and then do this exercise.

These are my Vision Points:

Vision Point 1:

Vision Point 2:

Vision Point 3:

Remember that all parts of you are working with you and God to create what you ultimately desire. Once you know what your role is, what God's role is and which parts of you are responsible for what, you merge onto the Super Highway of Life. Your life will feel as if you just climbed into a Ferrari and took off! You may wonder why you didn't do this sooner. Who cares? Enjoy the ride!

Getting Off the Motor Mind Track

When your mind is going in circles, it can be scary. It *feels* like you aren't in charge. It *feels* like things are spinning out of control. It feels like you are in a racecar being driven by someone else, and you can't lean over and grab the wheel. You feel this way because those mental laps you are taking around the track are made of mental energy. These laps create what look like strings in your mind. Pretty soon, it is as if the Motor Mind is playing with silly string. It can feel like bondage because you are all tied up on one track of thinking.

It feels like you are on one side of the Grand Canyon–the divide in your mind–and it is going to take a l-o-n-g time to get to the other side. In reality, you're right next to you and the solution. Your perception is skewed by the energy you are working under. Getting off the track is as simple as saying, "I'm making laps around the track, and I don't want to do this anymore" and choosing a new Vision Point or destination.

Let's say you are feeling bad about something you said to someone. Shame makes the Motor Mind go crazy. You replay the conversation in your head over and over again, reliving the feelings over and over, too. Instead of making another lap, stop and go to the questions above. The past is in the past. The only thing that can change your current, present moment is to decide what you want right now. Decide, create a Vision Point and give your Thinking Mind a job.

If you've been doing mental laps for a while, it is imperative that you release the mental energy. When I see these thought forms, as mentioned before, they literally look like tornadoes in the mind.

This energy is laps and laps around the track, and the circles lift like a funnel. Here are four easy ways to let these go:

1. **Move:** Get moving in a rhythmic way–walking, jogging, cycling, jumping, boxing, swimming, mowing.
2. **Meditate:** Imagine a hot-air balloon coming down and picking up the energy and floating away. This is not as effective as movement, but it can help manage the circular logic.
3. **Pray:** It never hurts to ask for help. Ask to be released from the crazy-making Motor Mind, and thank God for taking these thoughts away from you.
4. **Forgive:** Use The Power of Forgiveness Meditation (page 57). Forgive yourself and forgive others. This will help reset all of that energy and put you back on higher ground.

You are in charge of you. When you take ultimate responsibility for yourself, then it isn't 'him' or 'her' driving you crazy. It's you driving you crazy. Luckily, it won't take 10 days and a U-Haul to get you from here to there; it just takes awareness and willingness to jump off the track once you realize you are on it.

Problem Creating vs. Conscious Creation

One of the hallmarks of people who are living their best lives is that they naturally drift toward thinking about where they want to go and what they want to create. Instead of focusing on the problem at hand, they focus on what's next. You can do this, too. It's just a matter of increasing your awareness and realizing that wherever your attention is, so is what you are creating.

The Thinking Mind is the Clydesdale–your Vision Point. Whether or not you are being intentional, it is holding the focus for you and sending it to your subconscious to deliver the goods. *For this reason, it is vitally important for you to be sure that your focus is on what you truly want to create.*

Most of us are taught from the time we are tots to focus on what we don't want. "Be careful, you might fall." Or, "That's dangerous, watch out that you don't get hurt." Or, "Why did you make a bad grade?" The focus was mostly on what was *not wanted.* If you walk through life with your focus on what you don't want, then rest assured you are not alone, as most of us grew up with the same conditioning. Many people live in a perpetual state of commiseration talking to people who reflect back similar thoughts. You are not special in your problem-creating!

The reason questions that direct your focus are so helpful is that they are designed to carry you closer to a conscious creation versus creating more problems.

Does it really help for you to go back and forth in an argument with a friend? One of you says, "You hurt my feelings!" and the other says, "No, you hurt *my* feelings!" By pausing and asking a conscious creation question, you can cut to the chase and say, "Where do we want to go now?" In the union of deciding *together* to go somewhere, you can see that you love the other person and the other person loves you, and you are deciding to go into the future together. As you take the conversation to higher ground, each of you will be heard, which is what you really want when you are screaming at each other. Conscious creation shifts your focus on where you are going while holding you safely in the present moment.

The Motor Mind is the land of rehashing and going in circles. It is problem-creating. It focuses on the past and what is not wanted. "I feel bad, I feel bad, I feel…bad." The Thinking Mind can come in and say, "And what would you like to feel now?" Then it can go to the next level and take you there with focus.

If you don't do anything else in this book, this one thing can change your life. Focus on what you want, not on what you don't want. Create a habit of stepping over the muck and going straight to giving your Thinking Mind a job to do–create a new Vision Point.

Some common examples:

I Want	I Don't Want
To be acknowledged for my Truth.	*I'll never get ahead, what's the use of trying?*
Love on my own terms.	*To feel taken advantage of.*
A friend who listens.	*I'm sick of so-and-so not caring what I say.*

"You don't want me to have feelings!" she cried. "I'm hurting and you just want me to step over it and keep on going. Well, other people you work with might be able to do that, but I can't. I really can't, and you are hurting me by asking me to do it."

I listened quietly, allowing her words and energy to bubble forth. Then I spoke. "It's your choice how long you choose to suffer. We all have feelings, and healing takes time. Suffering, in my opinion, is a choice. If your feelings were taking you toward healing, I would tell you to be with those feelings, but they are not. They are taking you deeper into suffering. So my question is, 'How long will you choose to suffer?'"

It is a romantic notion to be so tied to another that you lose yourself. It is not a practical way to function in reality, but what does emotion have to do with reality anyway? Emotions are feelings with labels. Feelings alone do not have an emotional connotation. As you filter your feelings through your mind, an emotional equivalent pops up to match that feeling and you have a label for it–and that label is a certain emotion.

Working with your emotions requires patience. They are full of energy, not just the energy of today, but the energy of every other time you've had this feeling or experience. It's not only your husband who is standing in front of you asking, "How could you do this? What were you thinking?" It also your mother, your brother, your father, your second-grade teacher, your college professor, your first boss and your best friend from school. It's the collective experience of all of them that sets the emotion in motion and makes it that much harder for it to depart.

No one is saying you can't have feelings, that it isn't okay to grieve, that it won't take time to allow the flow of energy to move through you. This is a reminder that you are always in charge–regardless of outward appearances–and you can choose to be okay for now knowing that it's also okay when the emotion comes again. Fighting it only makes it worse, and when you realize it is you fighting with you, it will be easier to call a truce, recognizing it is okay to be 'fine' when you aren't supposed to be, and that you can be curled in a ball when you are supposedly on your way to being fine. You are where you are–just be sure it's a conscious choice.

Trap Doors of the Mind

A trap door is simply a false belief you have taken in to believe as Truth. It would take an encyclopedia to share the many trap doors available for you to fall through in your Thinking Mind. The tell-tell sign of a trap door is an 'all or nothing' characteristic. They spring from beliefs that have been accumulated over time. These trap doors are so common, it will be easy to relate to them and know in an instant when you are approaching one.

Trap doors are all about impossibility. If the soul is its counterpart of all possibility as a creation of God, the counter aspect holds the trap doors in its impossible orientation. Trap doors are good ways to find yourself falling off the path into a detour or distraction. They can often be the entryway to the ditch. Discovering which trap doors affect you is work that will be worth every second of effort you put into it.

I most often see six trap doors when I work with clients. There are many, many more. You are likely to know yours intimately. You'll have a chance to note them in a minute.

Comparison

More pain comes from this one trap door more than any other. No Truth can come from comparison because it is born from ego and judgment. The entire experience is judging yourself as compared to someone else. There's no way to compare yourself with anyone because where you are and what you are is exactly perfect for you right now. Comparing yourself to anything else is an open invitation for the Motor Mind to jump on the track. Let go of comparing things and you will find a lot of time and energy for more good in your life.

Perfection

The trap door of perfection says, "Everything else is perfect and I am not." It also can say, "I must be perfect or I am unacceptable." When you shine the light of Truth, you see that nothing is perfect and you are also imperfect. However, what you may not see is that all of this imperfection working together is a perfect creation for right now. The mess you are dealing with is exactly what you need to move toward what you want next. The 'disaster' you've just lived through is exactly what it took for you to see how amazing you are.

Earning Worth

The trap door of worth says, "I must *do* something to be worthy. If I do nothing, I am not worthy." If I do not match what my parents want, what society expects, what my spouse wants, I do not matter. When you shine the light of Truth on this, you will see that those who believe they are worthy are seen as high worth. Claiming worth is an internal process, not one that comes from others. If you don't believe you are worthy, no amount of others telling you you are will ever change that. You must know that by your very existence, God has made known your worth. Your very breath is what says you are worth something. Many derive their worth from helping others, which is another trap door. Your worth must come from within. When you give to others from that place, others will feel your worth and respond to it.

Who am I to...?

This trap door is a slippery slope indeed. It says, "Who am I to dare to be great?" "Who am I to consider I have something others want to hear?" Who am I to think I can be a ____________?" The trap door of "Who am I to…?" is related to worth and shows up in a way that says it's not okay to stand out; it's not okay to even *think* you are special. It moves between, "If I can't be somebody, then I guess I'm a nobody. Why even try?"

How?

The trap door of 'how,' whether it is "I don't know how" or "How do I do this?" can trap you indefinitely if you are not on the lookout for it. The Thinking Mind wants information, and when it doesn't have it, it can throw a tantrum until it gets it. This is a trap door that can send you on long wild-goose chases that find you going in search of information that you may not even *need*. 'How' is relative to your Vision Point. If you are going to build a house, do you ask how do I build this, or do you first decide to build the house? Most people stuck in the 'how' trap door are in the all or nothing–"I don't know *how* to do what I really want, so I will do nothing."

I Can't

This trap door is linked to insufficiency. The "I can't" trap door keeps you stuck before you ever get started. It's like shutting the garage door while you are trying to back out. It's a mind-numbing, frozen trap door that won't allow you to get moving. You won't even try from this trap door. You will live in the confines of what you currently know until you dare to move outside of this thinking.

Crystal Clear Clarity

Trap Doors of Your Mind

Which trap doors are you engaged in? Think about the drama in your life. Anywhere there's drama, there's illusion. Which trap doors serve you and are your favorites (they work splendidly to help you escape, deal and hide out)?

Which ones are you really tired of (these you have outgrown and are ready to release)?

The Receptive Mind, a.k.a. Vision Keeper

The Receptive Mind, also known as the subconscious or the unconscious mind, is the Vision Keeper. It is the part of your mind that is *really* in charge of all of your decisions. For example, Tara's subconscious was fully available and feeding her the energy of a new creation. Most of us believe our Thinking Mind is in control, when in reality it is the combined union of the Thinking Mind and the Receptive Mind that work together to take us to our future. Anyone who has ever 'decided' to lose weight only to gain even more understands that the will of the Thinking Mind alone is not enough.

The Receptive Mind is the place of creativity, energy and support. Without the Receptive Mind's agreement, the Thinking Mind is like a car running on fumes and three good tires. The Receptive Mind is the Vision Keeper because it holds the vision of what the Thinking Mind has brought into focus. This part of you is easy to work with. It just says, "Yes." So if you are saying, "I'll never get out of this. I'm in the worst place possible," your Receptive Mind says, "Yes, we are in the worst place possible."

I call the subconscious mind the Receptive Mind because it is a receptive vessel for all your requests. Not only does it hold our memories, but also it is the place that unites us with All That Is and connects us to EVERYTHING. It works amazingly well with mental pictures of what we want to create and feelings that tell us that what we want to create is possible. It is in the background, it is guiding our habits and actions–either closer to or further away from what our conscious mind wants. *It always says yes to what we believe and focus upon.*

This part of you holds a databank of information you have collected over a lifetime. Your parent's beliefs, your community's beliefs, your nation's beliefs–all are captured with no discernment as to whether the belief is needed. Everything you filed away from your life experiences is in there, too...'Don't yell at Dad after he's had a long day at work,' Or, 'Don't ask too many questions or people won't like you.' All your experiences have created beliefs that your Receptive Mind has meticulously filed away for you with all kinds of rules associated with these beliefs. *You* are simply a passenger in the Receptive Mind's car until you wake up and get behind the wheel through conscious choice.

When you come into contact with the receptive, subconscious mind in a more aware state, then you can get to know what you really believe–not what you *think* you believe in your Thinking Mind, but what you *really* believe in your subconscious.

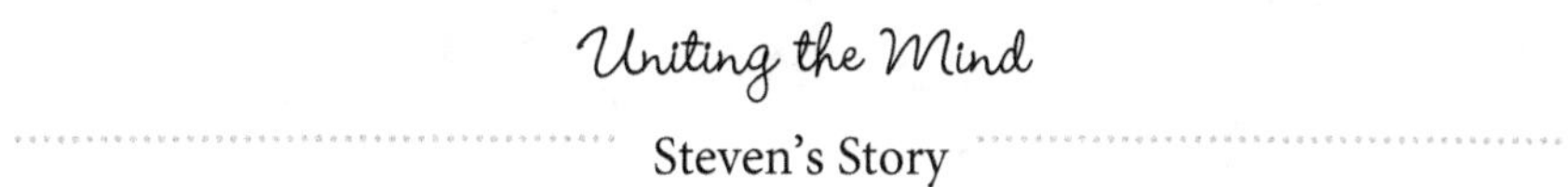

Uniting the Mind

Steven's Story

Steven, a great, all-American kind of guy, was frustrated in his business. "I don't know why I can't seem to go past the $7,500 mark for my consulting fees. I know there's a barrier there because I can feel it," he said, clearly frustrated.

"Agreed. This makes sense. What I want you to do is tell me what you really want."

"I want to make $10,000 for my consulting fees," he said confidently.

"Great, now say out loud: "I make $10,000 for my consulting fees."

"I make $10,000 for my consulting fees," he proclaimed with confidence.

"Now what comes after this? What do you hear in your inner voice?"

He was silent for several minutes, and then I heard a deep intake of breath followed by a resigned sigh. "I hear that I'm ripping people off and that only greedy people make that kind of money. I hear a bunch of other things, too. I know this is what I heard from my dad my entire life. It's him all over again."

"Wonderful. Ready to let it go?"

"Absolutely."

What Steven was dealing with was a classic conflict between the Thinking Mind and the Receptive Mind. Every time he tried to go to the next level, his subconscious would pull back and balk at asking for the higher price. If he managed to ask for the higher price, he exuded anything but self-confidence. Finally, after letting these belief s (and his dad's disapproval) go, he was able to more than double his fees.

True You Tool

Uniting the Mind

Think of something that is on your mind, perhaps something you want to change and haven't been able to. Use this technique when you are at an impasse and have no idea why you can't move toward an action or creation. Write it here:

Now, say what you want to create out loud. For example, if you want to be at your healthiest weight, say "I am a healthy weight" or "I am my perfect weight."

Now, note what comes to your mind *after you speak your* Truth. Write your thoughts here.

Say it again. Note the thoughts here.

And again.

And again, if needed.

You may need another piece of paper if this is a long-standing issue. You may do this more than 20 times. Don't worry about it. Just go with what comes. You are emptying the incongruent thoughts and beliefs. Now, say it again until you record a positive response such as: Yes, I am!

And another.

Now ask, "What is the Truth of this for me? What is my focus now? What is my first step?" Write your inspired action here:

Now, take inspired action!

Part of your mind is concerned with keeping things safe. If, like Steven in our example above, going against the many beliefs of your parents, your Reptilian Mind is pouring out warning signal after warning signal that says, "Alert, alert, moving into unsafe territory." Although the Receptive Mind *is* receptive, it requires the Thinking Mind's attention–and focus–for the Receptive Mind to shift belief. Remember that the Receptive Mind builds in new beliefs through affirming a new Truth and *experience*. This does not mean the experience has to be *your* experience.

If you believe all men are losers because your mother did, and then your best friend meets an amazing new boyfriend, marries and has a great relationship, your Receptive Mind could be open to a new belief or reality. Similarly, people who read books may adopt a new belief from knowing what *is* possible. When the Receptive Mind believes, and the Thinking Mind directs, the body can move to create what is true for you.

The Receptive Mind is an evidence-seeking missile. If you believe that people never get ahead, your subconscious will always be on the lookout for this. Soon your conscious mind is in the game noticing all the myriad of ways your Receptive Mind is delivering the evidence to your door. By understanding that it is all about evidence, you can work even more effectively with your mind to change or alter beliefs. What you believe, you will see over and over again. If you don't like what you are seeing, change what you believe. People often ask me, "Is it really that easy?" Yes, it really is!

Your Receptive Mind is always at your service; it's your best ally when it comes to reuniting with who you truly are. It always says yes. When you realize you aren't stuck with whatever was programmed in there over the years, you can consciously work with the Receptive Mind so that it can support the Thinking Mind. The two work together with the rest of you to serve you to be all you can be. You literally are designed to create anything you can hold your focus upon. Isn't that fabulous news?!

Your Body, a.k.a. The Peace Keeper

Your body is the link between the two parts of your mind. The conscious part of you may not have access to the Receptive Mind (unless you use a tool like the one provided here) and what it holds, but your body can act as the go-between. It can create a bridge for the parts of you to dialogue with each other.

I delight in how amazing our bodies are. Don't you? These amazing machines are flexible and determined to live no matter what they are given–or not given. I call the body the Peace Keeper because it is the place where we store excess energy, hurts, pains and other emotions until we can fully deal with them. By noticing where you hold feelings, you can quickly dialogue with yourself. If your mother calls and invites you to a formal evening and you notice you have a lump in your throat or feel sick to your stomach, your body is telling you something. It isn't about whether a situation is good or bad, it's just recognizing when you are responding to something so you can have full access to it if you like.

Your feelings are the language of the body, but they do not originate from your physical body specifically. They originate from the Receptive Mind's misalignment with what you are experiencing through your thinking mind. These feelings are a connection to what you may not realize. In short, feelings are a wonderful place to begin to honor who you are.

Your body is an amazing vehicle to take you to and fro. It is equipped with the latest technology. It will go through any type of weather, it will weather any storm and if you abuse it, it will graciously respond to kindness at lightning speed. Your body is the place where old hurts are stored until you are ready to retrieve them. If you find that as you reveal the *True You* that you are getting ill or are finding old injuries that you've forgotten about, realize that this is part of healing the old wounds. Instead of being upset your body is hurting, be thankful it is showing you how alive you are now!

"What is necessary to change a person is to change his awareness of himself."

-Abraham Maslow

Karen, a mother of six and a soul-full writer-artist, called to figure out 'what to do' with her family that was driving her crazy. I could see all six kids lined up and one looked lighter than the others.

"Do you have a daughter who has passed?" I asked her.

Her voice caught mid-sentence as she answered, "Yes, I do."

"She's here with us," I announced as I could see this young adult clearly and she showed me image after image of what was going on for her mother. "She loves you very, very much," I added as I saw her holding out a heart for her mother.

"So, I'm calling because I don't know what to do. These kids have so many problems. It's like I have to do and think for them!" she said in an exasperated tone. "She was always so responsible. I hoped she would come."

Her daughter showed me the Truth for her mother. She took me to see a little house in the country and I could see her mother writing there. "Do you want a place to write out in the country?"

"Oh, yes," Karen said with an enthusiastic lilt in her voice. "I've been dreaming of a place in the country where my whole family can come and get together."

"Karen, do you see that what you have created is exactly what you are dreaming of? Your house full of children is the result of your thoughts and your spoken words over time. You have created *exactly* what you want."

"I didn't want a house full of kids here with me!" she retorted. "And, with their problems, too!"

Suddenly, I saw the house in the country again. I saw her *alone* in the country. I knew instantly that what she truly wanted was space for herself and for her writing. The kids were part of her habit of putting everyone first so that she could *then* have what she wanted.

Her daughter showed me her siblings and showed me *their* Truth–they didn't want to be in this creation, either. They were there because they thought their mother needed them following this tragic passing. Each one had created a crisis that took them to their mother's home. Even the children's spouses were affected by the codependent co-creations!

"Karen, let go of worrying about everyone else for just a week, and give yourself time to write." I could see words flying in the air around her. You are a poet, an artist, a beautiful writer who has a need to express herself in this way," I urged. "It's okay to be happy. Your daughter knows how much you love her and she's here to let you know you've grieved enough. She wants you to know she is okay."

"But my children...they need help," she resisted. "They all have problems."

"Karen, see them as strong, capable kids and you'll strengthen the Truth in each of them that they can live their own lives. Let them go and they will find their way, and then you will have a chance to create for yourself and for them too. You can create from love and for the best."

"I still don't see how this works," she said grimly. "I wanted some help with my kids' problems."

I could see clearly that Karen's situation was exactly what she was envisioning–all of her family under one roof. However, because it didn't match the countryside vision in her head, she couldn't see that it was exactly what she created for herself and all involved.

"Trust yourself, follow your inner muse and write. That's where your answers are and when you find *your* answers, your kids will find *theirs*. We don't change others. We change ourselves and then others change around us."

Looking for answers? Karen's situation is like most. Life is a wonderful mirror and beautiful feedback loop that teaches us what we are paying attention to. Her soul wanted time alone to create and write. Her thoughts were consumed with being in the country. She longed to spend time in peace and quiet, but her habit of inviting everyone to go with her was alive and well within her. Without giving herself permission to have something only for herself, she kept dragging her family into the creation with her, and then when the family dutifully arrived at her house, then *they* were the culprits of all she was creating. They also served to be something to focus on *instead* of the writing her soul called out for her to do.

Self-awareness gives you the reins of your life so you can see in real-time what you are creating. By noticing your thoughts, your spoken word and a few other areas, you will soon be able to see that you truly *are* the creator of your world. Discovering that you can create effortlessly what you focus on is truly one of the most magical experiences you will ever know.

When you begin to believe that your focus creates your world and you trust God and the Messengers to bring unfailing support, your life will change in ways that make it hard to fathom life could be *so good*. You will know the moment you believe because your heart will swell with joy and you will feel the expansive support available to you in every moment. That's life as a lottery win!

The Mixed Bag of Self-Awareness

As you delve into the wonderful world of being present, you will find yourself immersed in hyper states of being. By this, I mean that you will notice things more intensely than you did before. The trees may seem more 'alive' and what was commonplace may now hold such beauty, you may find yourself moved to tears. This is common. No, you aren't losing it. You are only finding the divine connection available to every person on the planet. You are in the present!

You might find that you become very sensitive to ideas that once were background noise. Television shows that you used to watch may seem 'too violent' now. You might notice that you have more clarity around how you feel around people, in certain environments and what kinds of food your body craves. Your obsessions will die down and your consumption of mind candy likely will abate. Simply breathing may feel so 'new.'

As you develop more self-awareness, work with the following parts of you to increase your sense of Self. Choose one for a week or a month. Then move to another. Feel free to revisit this section often if you are feeling a little 'off.'

Your Body

Your body holds you in complete safety. It will take on whatever feelings you feel you can't deal with and it will send you messages when something is not right. Your body will try to get your attention in many ways from sending you a queasy feeling in your gut to flooding you with feelings of joy when you are squarely in the present. Take good care to listen to your body's language–*feelings*. If you ignore the feelings for too long, you'll find yourself feeling sick–an overdose of energy waiting for your time and attention. If you continue to ignore your body's call, that's when you will find an actual illness creeping in. Never fear, the body is resilient and it responds rapidly to your tender loving care.

True You Tool

Connecting to Your Body

Lie down or sit comfortably in a chair. Take in some breaths–deep into the lower part of the belly. Breathe in comfortably and now notice what part of your body hurts, aches or otherwise draws your attention.

Focus your attention on this area. What pops into your mind? What does your body want you to know? What is not resolved here? Try it again to show your Receptive Mind that this is not a one-size-fits-all exercise. What other part of your body wants your attention? Afterwards, note your thoughts here:

Your Thoughts

Your thoughts are a great tip-off to what's going on beneath the surface. Do you see a common pattern emerging? Do your thoughts have a theme? Do you see the same experience at work, in your relationship and with your five-year-old? Get to know your thought patterns, and realize that your thoughts are what you are focusing on and what you will eventually end up creating. *With your attention, you are creating.* This goes for thoughts, too. If your conscious mind is focused on "my boss is out to get me," then your subconscious mind will soon begin to hyper focus on the 'evidence' that this is true, and soon you will be responding to an entire experience created for you by you. To work with your thoughts directly, go to page 99 for a tool that can assist you to see your thoughts at work.

"I'm getting really, really bad feelings about my new boss," Staci said. "She acts like she likes me, but I can't shake this bad feeling. I ***know*** *something is going on." Her energy felt edgy, like a person who had consumed way too much caffeine.*

"What are you focused on?" I asked.

"I just told you. My boss is out to get me. I don't want to get fired. Didn't you hear me?"

"Yes, I did. And what I heard you say is that you are focused on creating getting fired. What can you do to focus on keeping your job or creating something better? What thoughts and actions go with a new focus?"

Staci's gift came in the form of giving herself a break. She was a self-proclaimed overachiever who was used to outshining everyone she worked with–and for. This new boss wouldn't have any of that, and as a result, began to remind Staci who was boss. As a highly intuitive person, Staci's body put her on high alert that her boss didn't like her need to 'outshine' everyone. A few weeks later, Staci quit her job and vowed to find a place where she could shine on her own terms and be valued for who she is. Her boss gave her the opportunity to look within for what is good already instead of needing to prove herself outwardly.

When intuition intensifies with your connection to the *True You*, you may pick up on things you weren't aware of before. If you find yourself in fear, this is a great time to recognize your power of choice. You can *choose* to face the fear. As children, we get used to dealing with fear in one of three ways–fight, flight or freeze. With choice, you can simply face the fear, deal with it head-on, and claim the gift it has in store for you.

How do you deal with fear?
Exploring Fight, Flight & Freeze

I am fascinated at how people really do know themselves intimately and choose to act as if they don't. When I ask someone what their cycle of going to the ditch is–how often do they take themselves there and how long they stay–people can tell me almost immediately, and often with little explanation as to what kind of answer I'm seeking.

The same is true for fight, flight and freeze. When you get scared, how do you deal with fear? Do you fight against it believing it is real? Do you flee from it trying to find comfort and solace from the boogey man? Do you freeze like a deer in headlights? Most people have one method of coping with a strong second they will turn to if the first can't be accessed.

By being aware of your coping mechanism, you can recognize you are in a place of illusion. Feeling that you need to run from anything is a good tip-off that you have entered into a place of false. The flush of wanting to flee is what sends most people into the ditch for a time out.

Use a current challenge or one from the past to explore how you deal with fear. Note your experiences here:

Your Spoken Word

The words that flow from your mouth are a good indication of what you are thinking. Watch your words and you will see your thoughts changing. All the parts of this mixed bag of your self-expression work beautifully together. Be aware of the slang terms people so often use today–*"My head is killing me." Or, "I'll just die if he doesn't ask me out."* Guard your words with your mind by bringing attention to them and ensure that what flows out is what *you* believe and want to *create*.

The more time you spend in your divine connection, the more God can work through you. If you've ever had an experience where you said something wise that you know did not 'come from you,' then this is an example of love moving through you for the other person. In this way, we all can be God's Messengers. If you want to see your life changing in miraculous ways, use this prayer:

True You Tool

Prayer to be of Service

Dear God,

I ask that I be used as an instrument of love and healing. Guide my words, my thoughts and my actions to be a reflection of your love.

Amen.

Your Mindset

Positive or negative, can do or can't do–all are related to your mindset. Your mindset is the accumulation of what you believe focused into a single moment. "That will never work for me" is just as powerful as "I can do anything." You choose what you believe. Your mindset is a big tip-off to what exactly you believe *is* the Truth–*your* Truth. Working with your thought forms and spoken words, you can quickly change your mindset with your focus. If you feel like nothing is possible, then change your words to "Anything is possible." When you find yourself saying, "It won't happen," change your words and thoughts to, "It could happen." These simple shifts send a ripple through your body and out into the higher consciousness. When you open your mind and heart, God says, "There's a door that is open to me where I can assist you."

Much of the work I do with clients falls into two areas: aligning the mind to assist and serve the heart and strengthening the connection to the heart to lead and express fully. Your mindset can literally keep your heart in bondage. Your heart is here to lead you, but it will never be forceful as it is only love. Your mind, on the other hand, can be extremely forceful when powered by the ego. This is one of the most important reasons why your mind requires a reminder to follow your heart.

Our minds often work much like a puppy–getting excited by "new" information, curious about anything and everything; easily distracted by new items. If you allow your mind to run the show, it is akin to putting a two-year-old behind the wheel of your vehicle. To strengthen your mind's support of the heart, commit to retraining your mind to look to your heart for answers. When you aren't sure of something, ask your heart and then allow your mind for support.

By connecting to your heart for focus, you instantly tap into your subconscious for support. You bypass the Thinking Mind and access God's love and wisdom. With practice, you can do this and you'll find yourself knowing from the place deep within that truly does know it can access any answer.

True You Tool

Affirmations

An affirmation is a statement you use to impress a new Truth on your subconscious. You literally use these statements to 'affirm' a new Truth. You can use affirmations to bolster a new way of being. If you've already worked with the other clearing tools in this book, then an affirmation is simply a tool to infuse new energy into what you choose to believe.

Create an affirmation by choosing a statement that supports how you most want to *feel.* Remember, creation is accomplished *inside* your heart–not in your head. This is about *feeling* great.

Old Way of Speaking to Myself	New Affirmation
Example: *This is too hard. It's no use.*	Example: *I can do this!*

Some people post their affirmations around the house, in the car, on the mirror. Some record their affirmations and listen to them at night. Use your imagination and go with what feels best to you.

Your Vision

Do you have a vision for yourself? For your life? No one has to know what your vision is–it can be completely between you and you. Be bold and create a vision that takes your breath away. Begin to allow it to permeate your being so it can take root like a beautiful, lush flower. As you write, write from the place in you that knows who you *truly* are. Be the person you know you are and you want others to experience. That may not be your reality now; it doesn't matter. Your vision is born inside of you–it's always available to you.

Your vision might be akin to your story from page 85 (see *My Story).* Usually, your vision will be something concrete or abstract. Some people see themselves in the abstract while others see themselves in motion. Let your vision move you. If there's no feeling in your vision, then you are not in your *True You.* You may also want to work with who you know you really are at your core as your Truth. Do what feels best.

Right Here, Right Now

Your Vision of Yourself

When you think of yourself, you see yourself as:

A True You Tale from the Queen of Dreams

Back in early 2005, I prayed incessantly to receive a vision of what my purpose is. I kept pleading with God for just a little peek of what I was here to do since I couldn't seem to figure it out the big picture myself. The answer was given to me, as requested, on an ordinary Thursday morning. I put my headphones on to meditate, and without a moment's notice, my mind started filling with images clearly outlining my life in three parts.

As I saw these flashes of the vision called "my life," I burst into tears with the feeling of unworthiness that I felt in every part of my body. How could I be asked to do so much? Who was I to do these things? And, how on Earth was I going to accomplish all this? Immediately the entire vision seemed overwhelming to my Thinking Mind.

I felt so much love at the same time I felt so much unworthiness. Somewhere in the middle of these feelings, I knew what I saw was true. It felt true. I dragged myself to the shower and continued to see more and more of the vision. I knew I had asked for this beautiful gift, and here I was crying in the shower saying, "I can't do all of this." My mind literally split as it tried to comprehend "how," and then I heard a heavenly voice say, "You will be given more help and support than you could ever begin to ask for–do not worry."

Since that time, the tools in this book helped me free my heart. Each one was created as I asked for answers for myself and for clients who came seeking themselves. If I can move toward a vision that seemed impossible to realize, so can you. Oh, and I've also had the fortunate opportunity to talk to others who have had similar experiences with their life purpose visions, and this feeling of 'being too small' for God's vision of you seems to be quite common. Stay faithful. You were born ready for the vision of who you really are! ♥

Your Values

Your values align with you at your core. Who are you? What do you believe in? What are you passionate about? What is your most urgent concern in the world? What do you want to be remembered for? What will people say at your funeral? What do you stand for? What are your personal standards?

These questions help you to determine what matters most to you. To download a form with a long list of values to choose from, go to http://www.TinaFerguson.com/mbp.

My Top 10 Values

1. ______
2. ______
3. ______
4. ______
5. ______
6. ______
7. ______
8. ______
9. ______
10. ______

Your Energy–What Are You Transmitting?

The residue you leave behind is your energetic footprint. A good way to know what you are transmitting is to look around and see what you are experiencing from others and what you feel moment to moment. Are people cheerful and friendly toward you? Do you find people hostile? Is it somewhere in between? Is your energy excited? Is it tired? Does your energy invite people who complain? Do you join them? Are you a helper in the world where people are drawn to you to help them, even at a store where you do not work? Use the space below to jot your ideas in stream of consciousness:

I once worked with a woman who exuded the energy of busy bee, exhausted mother and wife. Her busyness was not at all the energy her soul transmitted, but the buzzing of the busy bee 'noise' in her energy enveloped the peaceful, loving Presence she carried within her heart. The *True You* is always present; however, if you are spending only moments in the *True You*, then you may be attracting people who reflect the parts of you that are transmitting a louder signal.

Your energy might be a mix of many things. Be honest about how you feel. What you feel inside is what you transmit to others around you.

Crystal Clear Clarity

Energy Awareness

Share three experiences you had in the last week with others that made an impression on you. Be specific and detail how the person interacted with you, what you said, the feeling you had with this person and how you left this person. What do you notice about your experiences?

Your Noticings

The only way I can describe this part of your awareness is to say, these are the items in day-to-day life that 'grab' your attention. Your noticings show you what your subconscious has said 'yes' to. By noticing what you are noticing, you can then know what your attention is focused upon. This is a backwards way of recognizing what your focus is, and works very well. The *True You* is always calling you home. Noticings play a big role in working more consciously with your Receptive Mind.

A client once shared that she was 'bored' with life, but could not, for the life of her, figure out how she could feel bored when she was so busy with a thriving business, a new husband and good friends. I asked her, "What's been trying to get your attention? What have you been noticing that is out of the norm for you?"

It took her only a few seconds to say, "Mexican and Thai food restaurants. I notice them constantly."

"Do you eat at these restaurants often?" I asked. "What's special about these foods for you?"

"No, I don't because my husband doesn't like spicy food. I love these foods with their spices and flavors. I enjoy the exotic feeling I have when I eat these foods."

"Great, so when can you have lunch at these restaurants with a friend? It sounds like your desire for spice in your life is making its way to you through your taste buds. Follow yourself there and see what else shows up for you."

Your Actions

Actions are where the rubber hits the road. "Nothing happens until something moves" is a wise quote attributed to Albert Einstein. A thought is the seed of an idea that turns into the spoken word that turns into tomorrow's actions, which become your future creations. What are your actions telling you about your beliefs and your thought patterns?

The more your thoughts match your vision of yourself and how you act in the world, the more *you* can be you. If you have a grand vision of yourself, but your thoughts continue to be self-defeating, it is likely your actions will be a cornucopia of your misalignment. You might see yourself taking grand action one day and the next day looking for reasons why you can't. Your actions reveal what you believe inside–take a closer look to see where you can connect to your *True You.*

Crystal Clear Clarity

Moving in Action

I could be more deliberate in taking action. T/F

If true, I can do this by:

My actions reflect my highest values. T/F

If I could change one thing about the way I take action or don't, it would be:

Your Habits: New Habits Create New Experiences

Actions and distractions are supported by habits. Habits can serve or enslave. Have you outgrown some habits? Do you want to add some other habits to your life? Choose new habits and you will see new experiences emerge from them. Your life, your choice, your habits!

This program works at a deeper level, so once you identify these, there's no need to run out and try to 'make' them happen. By developing awareness around what you consciously choose, you can decide to let go of some habits and create others and then watch yourself put these into play–without 'making' something happen.

Habits That Serve Me	Habits That Enslave Me	Habits of Others I Want to Create
Ex: *Arrive 5 minutes early for all my appointments.*	Ex: *Always say yes to requests. Afraid to say no to others.*	Ex: *Politely decline an opportunity without excuses and guilt.*

Your Support Staff: Recognizing How Abundantly You Are Supported

No one creates in a vacuum. No matter how unique you think you are, no matter how amazing your ideas and dreams, God is always feeding you. You aren't the only one who assists you in creating your life. The amount of effort you put in is in direct proportion to how much you *believe* you are the one who must 'make things happen.' Remember, Easy Street is about collaboration.

There's no way you could create all by yourself–even if you tried. You are indelibly connected to everyone and everything all the time. How often you reach into the higher consciousness for inspiration is up to you. When new ideas surface at the same time, it's the cosmic soup that delivers similar energy and answers to seemingly unconnected sources. Even the remotest inventions have found two people who had the same idea at the same time. From Edison to Einstein, the higher consciousness was alive and well. This powerful resource is available to you, too.

As you begin to know your life is worth living fully and to believe that it is entirely possible to realize your dreams, remind yourself that you are never, ever alone. Support is a simple prayer or request away–*always.*

Crystal Clear Clarity

Acknowledging Your Support Systems

Take a moment to acknowledge and express gratitude for your support system. No matter what your belief, it's likely you have been supported by the inspiration of those who have gone before, by religious figures, by world ideas and people who love you. Open up and declare your support systems now.

Support Systems in This World	Support Systems in the Unseen World
Example: *Best Friend, Sue*	Example: *Jesus*

Conscious Connection

We've already talked about your conscious connection to the present through your body. The following three areas allow you to make conscious connection to God and All That Is. Of course, that's where you'll find the deepest connection to yourself as well.

Breath

The lungs hold the breath of life. You can go without food, without water, but without breath you could not survive more than a few minutes. Your breath can bring you to the present moment instantly by simply tuning into your inhale and exhale. In and out, in and out...you carry within you instant access to everything. When you breathe, ensure that you breathe deeply into the lower part of your lungs. When you do this, you will find your lower belly just above your pelvis rising and falling. If you ever find yourself anxious, focus in on your breathing and allow the breath of life to guide you into this present moment.

Meditation

Meditation is the process of making an intentional connection with God. It is the receiving side of a conversation with God. Meditation helps you train your mind to be still so you can actually hear from God and the Messengers. This time with yourself allows you to take a break from a chattering mind, and be open to receive what is available to you.

Many meditation CDs make it easy to learn how to meditate. I suggest simply practicing for five minutes at a time focusing on your breath. Breathe in and then out, in and out, and then let the thoughts float in and out. If you try to force your thoughts out, they will continue to come. Just allow them to float out. With practice, you will be able to focus your mind and attention and your thoughts will subside. Meditation is much like exercise; you get what you put into it. This form of communion with God is like no other, though, and I encourage you to give yourself the gift of this amazing connection. I can't imagine my life without meditation–that's how rich a gift it is.

Prayer

With an open heart, prayer can send up a sprinkling of you to God and the Messengers. When you are present, asking in prayer for help, you can count on an answer coming to you toot sweet! Prayer is different than meditation because you are actually talking *to* God.

In prayer, you can ask for help, ask for guidance, express your gratitude, release your worries and simply share your ideas. Prayer is like any other conversation you have with another person. You say something and then you listen for the other person to respond. You 'listen' by focusing on your heart. That's where you will 'hear' God's response. You might hear a response in meditation, too, but in deliberate prayer, you will find answers come to you in the moment as well.

A True You Tale from the Queen of Dreams

For me, I've been talking to God since I was a little girl. I haven't always known how this conversation worked. I just knew it did. During school, I would whisper, "God, I don't know the answer to this question." Suddenly, the answer would appear with a light on top of it. "Thanks, God."

Later, as my concerns turned to bigger things such as a job, I would stop in the middle of my college campus, "God, I need a job." I would hear a response such as, "Go to the campus career center." Not knowing such a thing existed, I would take fast action to find it. Once there, I asked how to get a job, and then would be pointed toward a job board. As I looked at the board, I could see one job posting lit up and that's the job I got.

When I've felt down and wanted to lift my spirits, I would whisper, "God, I don't know what I need, just send someone." A few minutes later, a person would call and say, "I just had a feeling I needed to call you." Now, I'm grateful I can respond to God, too. ♥

Remember your divine connection and your *power* to call upon God for answers in all things. You are treasured more than you could ever imagine. A whisper from your heart can be heard in every corner of God's Universe. You don't even need an iPhone for that! If you can make a request, you can connect.

Self-awareness is ultimately the gift you give yourself. It makes life a more colorful, richer experience. Your relationships with others intensify. So does your relationship to everything around you, including yourself. It's a juicier, more delicious way of experiencing day-to-day life.

Section IV

Living Life as a Grand Adventure, a.k.a. Welcome to a Whole New Way of Life

"Many of us are waiting for the itinerary, the map and the packed bags to arrive before we begin living this grand adventure called life. In truth, we each have a built-in GPS system that can take us on an adventure of a lifetime. If only we dare to begin the journey."

-Tina Ferguson

Chapter 9

Relax, We're In The Soup Together—Venturing In To New Worlds

"One is loved because one is loved. No reason is needed for loving."
–Paulo Coelho

The following lyrics were written by Chuck Brodsky (www.ChuckBrodsky.com), a folk singer with a knack for putting into words the feelings we have in our hearts. This song, *We Are Each Others Angels*, so lovingly and gently reminds us that we are all in this world together, and when we stick together, we support and hold each other up. If you ever feel lonely, think about all the angels who have walked with you during your life, and consider how you've been an angel to others, too.

We Are Each Others Angels

I hope I see you later–'cause it's time for me to go
That's my ride that just pulled over–and it sure was good to know you
So go answer your calling–go and fill somebody's cup
And if you see an angel falling–won't you stop and help them up?

We are each other's angels–we meet when it is time
We keep each other going–and we show each other signs

Sometimes you'll stumble–sometimes you'll just lie down
Sometimes you'll get lonely–with all these people around
You might shiver when the wind blows–and you might get blown away
You might lose a little color–you might lose a little faith

We are each other's angels–we meet when it is time
We keep each other going–and we show each other signs

Thank you for the water–thought I was gonna to die out here in the desert
but you quenched my thirst
Let's break a little bread together–I've got a little Manna – it was a gift
From someone who was passing by and offered me a lift

We are each other's angels–we meet when it is time
We keep each other going–and we show each other signs

Do you feel angels have lightened your load along the way? What about the angels who taught you lessons and beckoned you to be more of who you are? They come in all shapes and sizes, and they don't always *look* like angels. But there they are and here you are, and we are all in the soup together. Have you been an angel to someone else? Lent a helping hand when you've felt called?

The promise and benefit of returning to the *True You* and plugging back into your passion is that everything gets infinitely easier, including relating to those around you. We are in the soup together by design; it takes all of us working together to live our best lives.

Some clients who are less familiar with looking inside can work through their relationships with others to reveal the *True You.* That's what this chapter is all about–working with feedback from those around you to discover the Truth. You'll find that many of these tools look like those in other chapters. The only difference is that they use an external reference point of others to reflect back to you areas where you can reconnect to the *True You.*

One of the greatest gifts on the planet is the family dynamic. Nowhere else is there as much opportunity to heal–both ourselves and others–as there is in the family dynamic. Love relationships commit two people at a deep level for unveiling the Truth, and when two people fully commit to each other, this kind of love can transform not only the people in the relationship, but the many people connected to it, including children and families of origin. The resources available to work together are powerful indeed. See for yourself!

By the time you return to your Truth–to the love you are inside–you won't believe anything else, either. Once you are on higher ground, there are some ways you can work with others to share the *True You.*

I've often seen people turn over a new leaf and go into hyper ego mode. They are empowered, they know what they want and to heck with everyone else. The feeling of actually knowing–possibly for the first time–who you are and what you want can be intoxicating. But at what price? As you move through reclaiming your power, some people will no longer fit with you. When you come from a place of Truth, these shifts will happen naturally. People who are not a fit will drift away–you won't have to kick them out. It may be sad to see people moving away, but keep in mind that new people will come in. Those that stay may be with you to question you, to see if you have really made your choices and to love you as you grow. And, remember the rescuer trap–now that you know yourself, people who want to know your secrets will ask you for them. Share with those who seek you out, but let others live their lives. No one enjoys someone who all of sudden has 'all the answers.'

We are all in the soup together, helping each other move to more of what we are in Truth. Remember that the greatest gift you can offer to the world is your *True You.*

When You Own "Me" Then It's Easy to Be "We"

By accepting responsibility for yourself and your choices, it's much easier to be with others. Suddenly you move away from looking outside of yourself for something to complete you, make you happy or prove your worth. By looking first inside yourself and God for the answers, the 'we' falls into place.

In every relationship–parent-child, spouse-spouse, friend-friend when you are dissatisfied, you can transform the relationship by focusing on your own happiness *first.* The transformation may help the other person grow or go. You never know, but the outcome, with your focus on your wholeness, can be integral to who you truly are.

For most of your life, you likely have thought you had to go out in the world to make a change or to try to change something. Anytime you are looking to change another person, stop and go stand in front of the mirror. The person that most wants your attention in that moment is *you.*

This is counterintuitive because you have learned to believe that you *go* and *make* something happen. Isn't it great news to know that all you must do is *first* look in the mirror and *decide* what you most want and then *only* take the actions you are inspired to take? This alleviates the whole cycle of 'I'm going to go handle this!'

"I always looked for someone, or something, to make me happy. When I was little, it was my daddy. When I got older–in my teens–it was food. Later, I turned to drugs and alcohol. I don't really know what I was searching for or why I felt such emptiness. All I know is that I can't remember a time I felt up to par and okay with who I am. I married young, and my husband didn't make me happy. The two kids we had didn't do it either, although I do love them very much. I divorced my husband because I felt like he was the problem, but of course, it was me all along. I think it was when I woke up next to my second husband, who is a prince and felt like I wanted to leave because I wasn't happy, that something hit me in the head. The only thing all of my experiences with being unhappy had in common was me. It was me all along. The others were just along for the ride. I knew at that moment it was up to me to make me happy. That was the beginning of a whole new way of life."

–Nancy, age 46

Right Here, Right Now

Increasing Trust

Use this form below to reveal areas where you could be more 'you' if you could trust more. Let your intuition guide you to the answers. Go with the answers that pop in your mind.

Person or Loved One In My Life	Percent I Feel I Am Myself When I Am With This Person	What Stops Me From Being True With Him/Her? What Could Improve This?
Ex: *Wife*	Ex: *93* %	Ex: *She could listen to me better.*
	%	
	%	
	%	

Person or Loved One In My Life	Percent I Feel I Am Myself When I Am With This Person	What Stops Me From Being True With Him/Her? What Could Improve This?
	%	
	%	
	%	
	%	
	%	

Crystal Clear Clarity

How You Relate to Others

In what areas of your life have you blamed others for your own dissatisfaction? What's the Truth? What does this mean for you today?

Let Go of Competition and Embrace Cooperation and Collaboration

A great deal of the way we relate to others is based on ideas installed at an early age. Competition for children is as natural an experience as walking. If you were the oldest child of four kids under five years of age, you likely had some challenging experiences getting enough of your parents' limited attention. Or, what about if you were in T-Ball and you had the strikeout that lost the game? Many experiences may have shaped ideas of 'not enough,' 'I've got to get mine before they get theirs,' or 'I can work hard to get my share.'

When you unleash the *True You*, many things happen. Instead of being something you aren't and dealing with the litany of experiences that come to you that reflect what you aren't, you get to relax and be yourself. You get to enjoy your days and see new people who reflect your vibrancy. Your experience moves to cooperation and collaboration as a natural extension of being with those who are in alignment with who you are, and by being what you are–love. It doesn't mean every day is a walk in the park, free of issues, but it does mean that most everything is easier because you are working with the flow instead of against it.

While friendly competition to do your best and make a game out of life can be healthy, the need to win at all costs can contaminate the Truth between two people. Knowing what is most important to you can help you step over and past needless competition or address competitive beliefs that no longer serve you.

Set Clear Boundaries

When you know what you need and who you are, it's easier for you to ask for what you want and create strong boundaries that will give your relationships the support they need to flourish. In our world, the word 'boundary' can have a negative connotation. It may sound like you are saying you need 'space' from another person. Strong, clear boundaries help people respect each other and enjoy each other more. Irritation, upset, anger, frustration–these are signs that something is not settling well. If you find yourself experiencing these emotions, think about whether you have loving boundaries in place.

Adventures in the Ditch

"For the longest time, I didn't even know what a boundary was. Boundaries sounded like imaginary lines drawn down the middle of a room to tell someone to stay on that side while you stay on your side. I had no idea that strong boundaries were ways we can love ourselves. The idea of asking for what I wanted sounded scary, let alone establishing a space for myself to be my best. I think I finally decided a boundary might be a good idea when my friend dropped in on me without calling first one too many times on one too many weekends. I found myself exasperated and ready to blow a fuse. I couldn't figure out how she didn't know, but she obviously didn't have a clue. How could she? Every time she came over, I welcomed her with open arms and encouraged her to come in. I knew I didn't want to ditch the friendship so I forced myself to exercise these boundaries so I could preserve my own sanity and our friendship. To my surprise, I was able to explain to her how it was important for me to have 'alone' days. She instantly understood it was something I needed for me; this wasn't about her. That experience helped me establish boundaries with others. Now, I can't imagine not establishing what I need."

–Debbye, age 46

Your Relationships

One of the most loving things you can do for yourself and others is to set clear boundaries about how you will treat each other. This may include how you talk to each other, how much you share of yourself with another. A boundary is an agreement you make between you and another person that ensures each of you is treated in a way that mutually enjoyable.

Person or Loved One in My Life	Boundaries in Place? Yes/No	What Could Assist? Action Needed?
Ex: *Mother*	Ex: *No*	Ex: *Let mom know I'm not talking about my marriage with her or discussing my children's challenges.*

Create Clear Agreements

Agreements are the commitments we make with and to each other. Most of the language we use to communicate is unspoken and created with tonality, body language, facial expressions and gestures. Is there any wonder that agreements might sometimes get a little *messy?*

Agreements can be direct or implied. A direct agreement may sound something like this:

Woman: *"Will you go pick up my dry cleaning today?"*

Man: *"Yes, I'll do that."*

The commitment between two people is clear and concrete. Even better is that it has a date assigned to it–*today.* Implied agreements are sticky and these are haphazardly created every day. An implied agreement may sound something like this:

Woman: *"Do you plan to go by the dry cleaners?"*

Man: *"Yes."*

The *implied* agreement is the man is going to go to the dry cleaners at some point. It's not known what the woman wants the man to do at the cleaners–pick up or drop off. Between lovers, between bosses and subordinates, between parents and children, each day we work with implied agreements.

By creating clear agreements, it is easier to ensure you are connecting with others and that the connection and agreement is clear.

Once you make your agreements, commit to honoring them. If you can't meet your commitment, be sure to address it quickly and clean up the situation. I believe most people are kind and forgiving if they are treated with respect. When you find yourself forgetting an agreement such as an appointment you didn't put on your calendar, be sure to address it quickly and truthfully. Don't go to the Motor Mind, just own it and act on it. What's done is done and you can easily ask for forgiveness. Remind yourself that everything is perfect, and there must have been a reason for the lapse.

A Gem From the Queen of Dreams

I once had a client whose appointment didn't make it to my calendar. I received a strong email from her, and I felt awful for about 30 seconds. Then, I emailed and shared with her my deepest apologies. I then felt inspired to ask if I was the only one who was not committing to her. I asked, "Has this happened with other people as well recently?"

She told me that the same thing happened with the doctor, another person and another service provider earlier that week. "Ah," I said, "Then this is something that you are holding for yourself. How are you not committing to yourself?" The lapse had actually opened up a deep conversation about truly committing to what she most wanted in life–herself. Face your lapses knowing that every one opens up a chance for the divine to work through you. This moment is perfect, remember the gift in each present moment. ♥

Create Healthy Agreements

Implied agreements don't go away. These are the agreements hanging around in the back of your head, regularly reminding you that they need attention. The only way to clean up these agreements is to honor them by fulfilling, cancelling or creating a new agreement.

Person I Am in an Agreement With	Messy or Implied Agreement	Next Step
Ex: *Sister*	Ex: *Expects me to lend her money when she needs it.*	Ex: *Let her know that she will have to come up with a different plan for money.*

Person I Am in an Agreement With	Messy or Implied Agreement	Next Step

Crystal Clear Clarity

Releasing Old Agreements & Accompanying Energy

When was the last time you made an agreement with someone that you did not fulfill? What was it? Was it direct or implied? If you are still harboring guilt, use The Power of Forgiveness (page 57) to let it go! If you've been married or in a partnership for a long time, is it time to revisit old agreements?

Heal Old Wounds

Uniting with the *True You* is about coming back to the Truth that you know you are here to express so you can be the fully realized expression of that which you already are. Being in action and moving in positive expectancy toward what you are creating can shift you and allow the *True You* to be expressed.

Still, even with increased self-awareness, as you move and act, there will be old wounds that will come to your attention. You will be more aware of the wounds because they resemble open sores around the areas that cause drama in your life. If you wince when someone says something about your being talented or you feel sick to your stomach when someone talks about the person who is perpetually late, your body is talking to you. It's your chance to take out the residue and let go of the stuff that holds you back from shining brightly.

Over time, you will experience less and less of these feelings, and yet by moving in action, you'll get to experience all your life has to offer you in the here and now.

Right Here, Right Now

Naming Old Wounds

Trips to the past are great for uncovering old wounds. What is in store for you in the past? What are you retrieving there? What holds your attention? What says a lot about what is important to you?

Wound	How Often Do I Think of It? Moment to Moment? Daily? Weekly?	On a Scale of 1-10, Am I Ready to Make Peace With This?
Ex: *I'm not good enough.*	Ex: *Daily*	Ex: *10 – I'm past done with this!*

A Pearl from the Queen of Dreams

"I can't think straight. I think about what I want, and then right behind it I think of the past and why I can't have it. I'm terrified that people are going to find out about me–about my past. It's like I am consumed with avoiding this. What is wrong with me? Why can't I stop thinking about this stuff?"—Angie, age 48

The 'stuff' Angie was carrying around were wounds that were more like huge boulders on her back. As much as she wanted to move forward, she couldn't because of the shame she carried around from past experiences. Making peace with the past allowed her to put the past right where it belonged–in the past. Then she was able to take the lessons and forgive everything else–most importantly, she was able to forgive herself. ♥

Embracing the Truth

Now, take a look at any wounds that keep attracting your attention and answer these questions for each. This will assist you in seeing these experiences differently.

Wound	Truth of the Situation	What Can I Learn From This?	What is The Gift In This?
Ex: *Not good enough.*	Ex: *I am great at many things.*	Ex: *This is a habit to think this.*	Ex: *This has kept me "safe."*

Clean Up Your Messes

Life isn't clean. It's messy. If you are like most of us, you have some messes that could use your attention. Maybe it's an actual mess in your house. Perhaps clutter is taking over your life–at home and at the office. Or, maybe your mess is in your body. Do you have some new habits to introduce or some old habits to let go of with regard to your health? Is your mess in your relationship? In your finances? Do you have messes in several areas? Are they related?

A mess holds your attention and brings a part of you to the current. Cleaning up your mess requires commitment, but it doesn't mean everything must happen *today.* When your Subconscious Mind is keeping a vision to clean up the mess, you'll find yourself cleaning out the garage not knowing why. Get all parts of you involved and celebrate along the way.

> *"Clutter has been a lifelong problem for me. I accumulate things, often unaware of why I'm buying something. This past year, I decided I would let go of one thing per day. At the end of the year, I will be down 365 things and that will be a great improvement on the clutter I have today. I might let go of a piece of clothing one day and a book the next–it doesn't matter what–what matters is the commitment to be in control of my choices around things."*
>
> –Betty, age 58

Address Your Mess

Take a moment and look at your life–what does your life have to share with you? What messes are asking for your attention?

Life Area	On a Scale of 1 – 10, How Satisfied Am I?	I'm Happy With...	What Needs My Attention is...
Love Relationship			
Self-love			
Friends and Family			
Health			
Finances			
Spirituality			
Home			
Career			
Other Self-care	Ex: 6	Ex: *Time I spend with myself*	Ex: *Wardrobe*
Other__________			
Other__________			

Crystal Clear Clarity

Facing the Dragon

Remember that you are not alone on your journey. We are all in this together. If you have been tackling an area for years, perhaps you would benefit from working with a professional. The professionals in the world are here because each one responded to an energetic call from those they would eventually serve. There's no shame in working with someone or asking for support. Write your thoughts about your biggest challenge here:

Take the High Road with Others

"What you are is what you get."

"Others are a mirror of what you are."

"Do unto others as you would have them do unto you."

Many sayings communicate, "you get what you give." When you think about our world and consider that we are all doing the best we can to varying degrees, it is clear that there's plenty of room to turn the other cheek. With your boundaries in place, your agreements clear and respectful, your wounds healing, you will find you have more space to give others the benefit of the doubt. You'll breathe deeply when someone flips you off on the highway instead of chasing them down to return the favor. If connecting with your Truth will do anything, it will give you moment-to-moment clarity of what is important to you.

When you share yourself with others and express yourself fully, you give others permission to do the same. You truly are the gift that keeps on giving. When you feel confident and secure in yourself, you easily can see the best in others and expect the best from them. Lo and behold, you will find that others don't disappoint. Expect the best and give others your best.

Be a Servant, Not a Fixer

Sometimes when we 'figure' things out and find something that makes our lives work well, we want to share our discovery with the world. The Ego Keeper–the Thinking Mind–without a good focus point, will begin fixating on seeing all the so-called broken people who haven't yet learned the lessons you have learned. This is the Fixer-Rescuer Trap. Well-intentioned people think they are 'helping' by offering help where it isn't wanted. As a result, these fixers unknowingly create victims and reinforce to these people that they can't do things for themselves.

The message the "victim's" Receptive Mind hears is 'You can't do it, let me do it for you.' The fixer believes she or he is creating the change and takes the power away from the person they are fixing. It is a sticky mess that can leave the fixer angry with the person she or he is trying to fix when the person doesn't follow through to being 'fixed.' It's a no-win situation and better left alone.

It's natural to be excited about your changes. In your excitement, you will undoubtedly be modeling a great new life. Remember what your essence does for those around you. Your true Presence assures others they, too, can choose to be happy. A person who serves offers help when it is *asked* for, and realizes that another person must do the work for her- or himself. This poem came to me as I learned this personally. It serves as a great reminder to serve from love, in the Truth.

A Fixer

A fixer has the illusion of being causal.
A server knows that he or she is being used in the service of something greater, essentially unknown.

Fixing and helping are the work of the ego.
Serving is the work of the soul.

When you help, you see life as weak.
When you fix, you see life as broken.
When you serve, you see life as whole.

We fix something specific.
We serve wholeness and the mystery of life.

Fixing and helping may cure.
Serving heals.

When I help, I feel satisfaction.
When I serve, I feel gratitude.

Fixing is a form of judgment.
Serving is a form of connection.

–Author Unknown

It's Not Personal

The super-sensitive ego can't stand to think about things that expose it as vulnerable or weak. The ego is invested in being right. When it comes to being with others, realize that most of your life you may have felt that it was you against the world. When you begin to connect fully to your heart and soul, you begin to see that it was you against you all along. It's the same for everyone else. So with this insight, be sure to keep in mind that nothing is personal. Even when things appear personal…they are not. Even when someone is in your face accusing you of something, it's not about you, it's about them. However, if you experience someone in your face repeatedly, it's back to you again.

The Motor Mind loves things that appear to be personal. When your Motor Mind connects to the Receptive Mind's memory bank of the last 10 times this happened, watch out–you could take a trip to the ditch in a New York minute.

The ego is invested in constantly knowing where it stands. Anything–good or bad–isn't personal. In my work, many people say wonderful things to me. I could take these in and believe this is what I am, but that would be a lie. I am not the remarks of others–good or bad. I am just what I am. It doesn't mean we can't appreciate the love that comes from these kind words. You can be grateful for who you are when it is reflected back to you. The idea here is not to be invested in these things because when they are gone, so are you. That's what happens when superstars go from top of the list to the bottom–they can't deal with it. To avoid this trap, just remind yourself often that you are brilliant in who you are no matter what you do or accomplish *externally*. Connect to love and the *True You* to come back to the present.

See the Best in Other People

Making the choice to see the best in others is easy. The habit of pointing out what isn't right or is wrong is just as easy to cultivate as the habit of seeing what is good in the world and in others. Neither is difficult; it's a choice. The more you see the best in yourself, the more you fall in love with who you are, the easier it is to share the love with others, and fall in love with them, too.

Encouraging others to be their best is a gift that costs you nothing and pays you exponentially in kindness. The more you can practice looking for the best in others, the easier it gets. Soon you will find yourself smiling for no apparent reason when you meet a stranger, eager to see what is unique about that person. This is something you won't know you missed until you have it.

Start at home, at the grocery store, with those you know, and those you don't. Remember the evidence-seeking missile of the Receptive Mind. It will find the opportunities for you. Soon, you'll be seeing more than the best in others, you'll be seeing the best in yourself, too.

Be a Dream Builder, Not a Dream Stealer

When you are in the essence of your true self, you are in a very powerful frequency that makes things much easier. The right people show up just when you need them, people are kind and abundance is a daily reminder of your new life. When you are in this beautiful new energy, it is important to be mindful when you slip back into your ego. We are all human and we all want many things that are attached to our ego. The ego can be judgmental and overly concerned with the world. Be mindful to be a Dream Builder for others–to hold a vision of who they are as pure love. Hold the light of peace and let the ego slide when confronted by another ego (a gift that tips you off when you go there). With your abundance and openness, allow the world to see the *True You*.

You can decide to be part of the problem or part of the solution. The heart and mind can work together for either. By focusing on the vision, you bring all the power you have and all the love *you* are to creating a better world for all. The highest expression of all is love. Be that love for yourself and for others.

Crystal Clear Clarity

The World You Create

T/F I'm in the habit of seeing the best in others.
T/F My friends and I routinely make comments about others behind their backs.
T/F I practice lovingly listening to others when they share intimate details and dreams.
T/F I am genuinely interested in what others are doing.
T/F I take the time to encourage people to do what they dream of or speak of.
T/F I feel that people encourage me to follow my dreams.
T/F I instantly am offended when others say things I don't agree with.
T/F I secretly feel envious when others are successful.

What thoughts do you have about the world you are creating? About the world in general?

Gratitude

Gratitude is one of the most powerful energies on our planet. When you express gratitude or appreciation, you connect to our Creator and to those who are connected to us through our gratitude. You lift up your heart to unknown gifts when you are grateful. You can speak your gratitude, record your gratitude in a journal and live your gratitude day-to-day. If you are ever feeling down or in the ditch, just pull out five gratitudes–speak them aloud to yourself and see how you feel.

This chapter began with angels and it ends with angels. Gratitude is key. You can never receive something without also giving something nor can you give something without receiving something in return. Look for all the things in your life that you have to be grateful for, including your health, your abilities, people who love you, the very breath you are taking right now. Once you begin focusing on what you are so grateful for, you will be amazed at how many other things there are to be grateful for!

Right Here, Right Now

Calling All Angels

Angel	The Gift They Were to Me	How My Life is Different	How I Was a Gift to Them
Ex: *Sixth Grade Teacher*	Ex: *Believed in me.*	Ex: *Began to believe in myself.*	Ex: *Thank her every year.*

Crystal Clear Clarity

My Angel Wings

How are you an angel to others? In what ways do you want to or already do serve others? In what ways are you serving in a way where you do not feel good and you can let go of your outdated agreement to serve? In what new ways can you serve?

When we lift up the hearts and souls of others by being a full expression of the love we are, we can't help but to also be uplifted in the process. Being an angel is a great–and easy–way to fly high.

Chapter 10

Living Life as a Lottery Win

"The privilege of a lifetime is being who you are."
-Joseph Campbell

"I know what I don't want," she said. "I don't want to go through more of this not knowing." Sofia's tone was matter-of-fact despite the feeling of frustration her energy conveyed. As an executive assistant in a large local financial firm, she was the glue that held everything and everyone together. She called because she was literally exhausted. Her body was getting sick every other week, and she wanted to get back the vibrancy of 'her youth.' She was only 42. Hardly old. But, as she put it, "very worn out."

Energetically, I could see gaping holes around her throat and heart. It looked like a war zone in those areas. I knew these areas indicated not expressing her personal Truth and not living her passion.

"What do you want?" I asked again, holding my focus and asking for more information. "Turn what you don't want into what you do want."

"I want to know why I am here," she said flatly.

"No you don't," I countered. I could feel the dullness in her voice. It was flat, lifeless. "What is it you *really* want?"

"I want to know that I'm special!" she spewed from the depths of her heart. "I want to know that what I do matters to people. That everything I do for others counts for something. I'm so sick and tired of plastering on a smile and acting the part of what I'm supposed to do."

I could hear muffled, choked-up tears following her release of the Truth.

"That is great, Sofia. How does it feel to admit that?" I asked.

Before she spoke, she drew in a long deep breath and then noisily exhaled it. "I had no idea that is what I wanted. Where did that come from?"

"Sofia, your soul has brought you here. You are ready to remember who you truly are and to start living a passionate life. Isn't that exciting?"

Her resolve back in place after the emotional outburst, she replied, "I've lived this way my entire life. I had no idea that I wasn't choosing it for myself."

"There is a part of you that is like this, but it is out of balance with the other parts of you. It is similar to how a diseased body part that isn't functioning puts more pressure on the other body parts to make up the difference. Your inner child is working overtime to please everyone and just threw a tantrum about it."

She laughed for the first time during our call. "I do feel like that. I remember when my mom died, I felt like I had to make everything okay for my dad. I went into good girl mode trying to make everything perfect. I just wanted him to smile again. I didn't realize that I just kept doing it. It is so automatic anymore."

"The first step is finding the point of creation. You've done that–good work! Now comes the fun part. What do you really want to create now?" I asked again.

"I don't know right this second, but judging from the excitement in my body, I bet it's not too far away, either."

Decide What You Want

How far away are you from knowing what you want? If you don't know what you really want, then I have some good news for you. You are like many others in the world. I rarely meet people who know *exactly* what would make their heart do flips in the air.

Sure, there are people who grow up knowing what they want; the majority, however, don't. Drifting from crisis to crisis in the victim mindset and the struggle to survive mentality, many people never get a chance to even *consider* what they want. Often, that's a great place to hang out if you don't want to contemplate your greatness. Who has the time or energy?

You are different. You are taking the steps to become more self-aware, to clear the space so you *can* consider what you really want and how you will create it. Additionally, you know you can have an amazing life and you will have plenty of support along the way.

Right Here, Right Now

What You Dream of...

When I Was a Kid, I Dreamed About…	When I Was a Teenager, I Dreamed of…	As an Adult, My Dreams Center Around…
Ex: *Swimming in the ocean.*	Ex: *Traveling the world.*	Ex: *Conservation/saving sea life.*

If You Don't Decide, Someone Will Decide For You

What do you want to drink? No doubt your mom asked you that many times. What happened when you couldn't decide or didn't really know? That's right, she decided for you. The same thing happens in life. If you don't know what you want for dinner, someone else will make the decision. If you don't know where you want to live, your spouse or some other life event will decide for you. If you aren't sure if the job you have is the one you want, a layoff could make the decision for you to find a new one.

Make no mistake, though, you *are* making a decision even if that decision is to be indecisive or not to make a direct decision. You *still* decide. There are no victims here. You decide in many ways, and the more you can see these subtle decisions as opportunities to make *deliberate choices,* the more you will feel connected to your life.

Here are a few ways people passively decide:

- Check out and focus on something else while another person decides.
- Give up on themselves, convincing themselves that they don't really get a choice.
- Tell a story to feel 'okay' about their current circumstance and indecision.
- Use distractions and detours that move them out of the present.
- Take a hike to the land of struggle, the future fugue or the swamp of the past.
- Throw themselves into "the ditch."

When you claim true responsibility for your choices, you will always see your options in front of you. You may not like the options available, but you will see them.

Crystal Clear Clarity

Making True Decisions

When was the last time you passively decided something? Describe the details here:

Where else in your life does this pattern pop up? If your example was at home, do you also do this at work? In your social experiences?

How is this serving you? What do you gain by not making an overt choice that puts you front and center for your choice? What are you giving up by not being true?

"I don't even know what I like to eat anymore," Cynthia told me. For years, this 50-something woman was so focused on the needs of others that she literally didn't know what she liked, what she liked to eat, what made her feel good, what dreams she might have. Her saving grace was her love of tennis–the one thing that kept her body and soul tethered together. "Come to think about it, I can't remember the last time I even chose the restaurant or what we had for dinner," she continued. "I never thought about this before."

–Cynthia, age 54

Make a Decision and Commit

Ready to decide what you want *for now?* You may feel discomfort at the thought of choosing something outright if you are out of practice. There are no rules here. You can start small. What would you like to drink? Make a conscious choice to choose Coke or Pepsi or vice versa. Want to play with something bigger? Try a new route to work. Change things up a bit.

Go bigger, and look around your life. What works? What doesn't? What is begging you to change it? Have you had the same hairstyle for 20 years? Why not start there? If you have the small things down, go even bigger and choose something else you've been secretly dreaming about.

Remember there is a distinct difference between *deciding to do something* and *thinking about doing something.* When you are thinking about doing something, you aren't committed to it. It is a wish your heart makes, but your feet don't get the message to move. It is living in the *idea* of the future. You may dream about it like it is a fantasy or you may wonder how it could ever be possible. Thinking about something creates thought forms that *could* take root, but deciding *and* committing to something moves you into *action* and the energy that can bring it to you.

When you decide, you are letting go of the how, which is God's domain. When you commit, you put all the parts of you in action with the actions of the Heavenly realm that is ever ready to serve you.

Steps to Creation

Imagine you are going to drive to the corner store to get a soda. What are the steps?

1. **Desire** – I want a soda to quench my thirst.
2. **Thought** – A soda sure would taste good right now.
3. **Decision and Commitment** – I think I'll go to the store and get one.
4. **Inspired Action** – You get up and go.

Now, as you imagine this scenario, notice: How does it feel? Is it solid, as if you know for sure you can do this? Is there any reason you can't create a soda? Is there any concern that it won't happen? This is the feeling of *decision* and *commitment.* The underlying energy is your knowingness of "I'm doing it." There's no question underneath; it just is. Your wants may not always contain elements where you know all the ins and outs of what you would like to create as in our example. You already *know* how to go *buy* a soda. That's easy. Faith serves you when you *don't* know how to do something; however, the decision and commitment part is just as critical *and the same* as when you don't know the steps.

Next, choose something you want to create. Come from an internal desire, and then make a decision and a commitment to have it knowing you don't have to lift a finger *except* when you get the nudge to go and take action. Just for this example, leave your Thinking Mind behind!

Write your creation here now. Be sure to be PRESENT–that's where your power to create is!

People fall into a mind trap when they make distinctions between small things and big things, and things they know and things they don't know. Asking for a small thing seems easier than asking for a big dream. *Yet, in God's world, every request is the same.* A healing is the same as asking for a primo parking space. A dream job is the same as asking for a raise in a job you don't really enjoy. The Thinking Mind loves to create stories and rules about how things work, so be sure you create what you want versus weaving fiction.

With your expanded self-awareness and the clarity that comes with knowing the *True You*, you will develop an ability to know quickly what you *really* want. Decisions will be easier, and the corresponding feeling of knowing will be accessible. If you come across a decision where you have fear, concern or doubt, use the tools discussed in this book to dig deeper to determine what holds your attention. Clarity + Knowing + Feeling Good = *True You* and your *True You* Life!

Be sure to keep in mind that the more you act upon your wants, the faster you will have more information that will either alert you that you are on the right track or that you may need a course correction. Either way, you are one action step farther along. Your feelings, as with everything else, are your clue to what you truly believe about your wants. Tune into your body when you decide, and let go of any outdated thoughts and beliefs that come between you and what you want!

Make Sure It's What You Really Want

I've had the fortunate experience to work with many people who were trying to determine what they wanted to create. Often, people *think* they want one thing when, in reality, they want something else. When you think of what you want, ask yourself these questions:

- What do I hope to get from this? This is *why* you want it. *This may change what you want.*
- Can I have this now? If so, in what way? *Go with the first thing that pops in your mind.*
- What's stopping me from having that? *This speaks to fears, limited thinking and beliefs.*
- What action comes to mind to take now? *Here's your next step!*

One of the easiest ways to distract yourself is to be caught in not knowing what to *do*. When you have decided–truly committed–to what you are creating, taking a step, any step, is energizing. If you don't know what to do, follow the one thing that comes to mind and has the most feeling and energy behind it, and do that first. Remember to trust!

Getting Clear and Specific So God Can Assist

When you begin deciding and committing to what you want to create in your life, you will soon realize that you are not creating alone. Not only do you create with your co-creators, but you also co-create with the Creator of All That Is. Your soul holds within it certain wants, desires, yearnings and dreams. You hold unique ideas and thoughts that you will express that are uniquely you.

If you have a desire to be rich, you might be surprised to learn that others do not share your desire. Some people have no desire to be rich. Others have a great desire to accumulate wealth. Some have a heart for serving others, while some may never want to serve other people. When we work from the Ego Keeper viewpoint, we believe everyone is like us. We see the world as a mirror image of what we think, what we believe and what we are seeking.

The more specific you can be about your creation, the better. If you have your heart set on a house, imagine the color of the brick, the inside layout, the backyard, the location, the direction it faces. The more specific you can get, the better it is for God to assist and aid you.

After you decide and commit to your creation–whether that is a new relationship, a house, a new body or a new career–begin to invite the pieces of you to co-create with God.

If you have no idea, you can request 'whatever is best for you right now' and be open to receive whatever shows up. The more you learn to trust, the easier this one is to use. You learn that God knows what your heart already desires, so the request is met quickly.

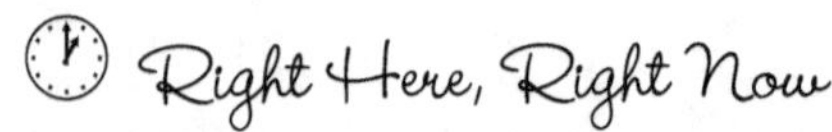

Creating in the Present

Invite your body to create with you. Imagine what this new creation is like. What does this creation *feel* like? Immerse your entire being in this new creation. What do you feel like? How does it feel? Take this feeling into every cell in your being.

Now, as you imagine this, close your eyes and invite a column of light to come into your inner vision or your feelings (you may feel it vs. seeing it). Notice where this column of light appears. Be mindful not to imagine a column–invite the column to appear…it *will* appear. Then notice where the column is. Is it in your experience with you? Is it behind you? Is it to the left or the right? This tool will help you see where you are allowing. Simply move over into the column and imagine your creation, taking it deep into your cells, letting go of the how and knowing it is done.

Note your thoughts here:

Breathe Life Into What You Are Creating

There are many ways you can bring your creation into your current reality. Be sure to come from a knowing place, not a 'pipe dream' energy. You know the difference. One has a decision behind it! You might create a vision board or a vision movie on your computer. You might take the first step toward that two-week European vacation by getting your passport and signing up for a Spanish class, knowing that the details as to 'how' you are going to get there are being handled. By taking action in a way you've been inspired to move, you'll set forth a ripple that rushes in to support you on every level.

Express your creation in any way that speaks to you. If travel to Argentina is on your mind, take Tango lessons. If you have a relationship you want to create, write down the attributes of your perfect partner, imagining them in full detail.

A Personal Story From The Queen of Dreams

A little more than 10 years ago, I sat at my computer typing an assignment for a freelance writing project. My mind wandered to my ex-boyfriend. We had broken up the year before, but I kept seeing him during holidays because I wasn't willing to commit to someone new. My heart pulled me to the Truth: **I was ready to be in a committed relationship again.**

I took a few minutes and wrote down a list of attributes for my ideal guy. Within 15 minutes, I went back to writing my article. As I pounded away on my keyboard, I heard a soft voice say, "Go to MatchMaker.com." I followed the guidance and found myself filling out a questionnaire that took 90 minutes to complete! I wanted to stop because there were so many crazy, silly questions, but I stayed with my inspired action.

A few days later, after learning how to deal with this new (to me) dating site, I came home and found myself magnetized toward the computer. I followed the pull and logged in. That's when Mark, now my husband, sent me an instant message. I didn't even know how to work the interface, so as I fumbled around trying to figure it out, I received an email, including a poem he had written. I read the poem and instantly knew: this could be the guy I've been looking for. We met a week later for a date. He came to my house the next day to make dinner for me, and never left. What I couldn't know is that on his end of the MatchMaker.com site, he 'decided' he was done with dating. He prayed and told God he was tired of looking. He asked that he be guided to 'the one' since he was only going to send one last email. That email found its way to me. The rest, as they say, is history.

Dreams do come true. *In addition to the miracle of our meeting, we both never thought we would have a child. After years of infertility with my ex-husband, I never thought I could have a child. Mark had endured a childhood accident that the doctors told him left him with a greater chance of winning the lottery than conceiving a child of his own. Three months later, we learned we were expecting our first child.*

You just never know what God has in store for you. I've found it is usually a lot more than we ask for ourselves! ♥

Expect It–Surrender Control

After you have done all the work to decide, commit and create, let it all go so God and the Messengers can usher in all you have *already* created with your asking. Just like going to get the soda, you don't think about going, double-check that you can drive the car, triple-check that you have two bucks in your pocket, keep going back and forth about the details of the soda, change your mind over and over again about the store you plan to go to. No, you decide and go. You let go, knowing that as you move, you can change your mind when you get there, and whatever you may encounter along the way will be handled–*just like it always is.*

Your illusion of control is just that–an illusion. When you surrender and let go, it is as if a legion of heavenly helpers comes to carry you along the path pointing out the best routes, directing the right people to you. Your job, at that point, is to show up and take inspired action.

This is a detailed view of your job description:

* Feel good in this moment, knowing you have *already* created what you desire.
* Do what you *do* know how to do to the very best of your ability.
* Give up trying to control how your creation will come to you.
* Give up trying to figure out 'how' you are going to create your creation.
* Give up your worrying and doubt about creating what you want.
* Give up your concern that you won't make it–affirm this or something better.
* Be grateful for what you have now.
* Love what you do, and do it with great enthusiasm and appreciation of your talents.
* Love your friends and family, and appreciate them for supporting you (or not).
* Know, without a shadow of a doubt, that you are supported by God and by Earthly and Heavenly Messengers.
* Expect things to happen, and keep an eye open for the things that *are* happening (your noticings).
* Stay present and focused only on the current inspired action you are taking in this moment.

Living in Positive Expectancy–Start Each Day on Solid Ground

Begin each day with gratitude. No matter where you are with your creation, be thankful where you are. If you are feeling like you are broke, be thankful for your health so you can work today. If you are feeling you are never going to catch up, be thankful for your ability to begin anew. Each day, jot down something you are grateful for from yesterday. Jot down several things if you like. The key is to begin your day in a state of grace and acceptance.

Let go. At the start of each day, focus on what you want to accomplish that day. Big buildings are built one stone at a time. Do what you know to do and keep your focus on those items. Begin with letting go of your need to force or control things by saying, "I don't know how all I am creating comes to me [insert your creation], I only know that what I ask for is given to me." When you say this, it will calm your mind and allow you to activate your subconscious to take over and look for those opportunities. Remember, your Receptive Mind always says, "Yes!"

This also invites God to work with you to bring to you the people, opportunities and resources you need to accomplish what you are asking for. This is very important because this allows you to be flexible and open rather than controlling and forceful.

Finally, be open to everything available for you. If you start each day by saying, "I'm open to all the assistance, love, joy and gifts available for me today," then you will find your days moving in the flow. And, last, but not least, invite the Creator and all helpers to work with you. Expect help to show up from everywhere and you will be delighted when it does!

"Destiny grants us our wishes, but in its own way, in order to give us something beyond our wishes."

-Johann Wolfgang von Goethe

The One Heart

If you are willing, you can intentionally and consciously connect to God and the one heart that connects us all. This is the place where all creators in the universe unite in the Unified Creation of All That Is. This means that any answer you ever want is accessible by uniting with the true heart within you. It means that you always have assistance available to you in a moment's notice. And, it means you are never, ever alone, no matter how much you may feel you are. The One Heart is the Creator's gift to you.

Your life can be richly enhanced by experiencing your divine right. I pray that you will open your heart to the many Earthly Messengers and Heavenly Messengers who seek to serve you. As you open to the miracles God has in store for you, I will hold the intention that you open to your gifts and you serve our beautiful world from the Truth of your soul.

Cutting the ties that bind, such as the mind that can't stop circling or the hurts that bring you to your knees, can be difficult, but the effort is exponentially rewarding. I know you can do anything you decide to do. I know you can create anything you can dare to dream and commit to.

What I Know For Sure

For as long as I can remember, I have known we are all connected. This doesn't mean I've always acted like we were. It doesn't mean I've always had the wisdom to delight in our connection. Rather, it means that on a very deep level, I've known that we are connected in a way that is *undeniable.*

The more often I am invited into deep, intimate conversations with clients and work closely with the Messengers, the more I see how connected we truly are. We each have more influence on others than we realize. Our thoughts, our words, our actions hold energy that we send to unaware recipients. We influence each other in so many ways and out of this comes a responsibility to be more fully conscious of what we are contributing to the "soup" we call life.

I know that you are here to be the fullest expression of what you are and to receive the fullest expression of that which you are from others. This fullest expression presents itself as love. This rich, complex and loyal love is one that you can only know by being that love.

For some time, I have been searching for what I am here to 'do'–my purpose so to speak–and on a very uneventful day a few years ago I received my answer after praying and asking virtually non-stop for months.

The answer was simple. I am here to love and to be loved. Just as you are. In its simplicity, the elegance touches me. What does this mean?

For me, I am gifted with the ability to see souls and to see soul gifts. I have been blessed to witness the hearts of many who held so much joy and love within them that their hearts appeared like the brightest star in the sky. Each one of you has a breathtaking landscape within you ready to express in our world. Your purpose is to paint your heart–your soul–on the world in whatever way makes you *joyful.*

Our word–purpose–is different from how the spirit world sees us. If there is no 'purpose' in the way we look at it, then what are these gifts for exactly? My clients have asked these questions as well.

My unseen spiritual teachers have answered my questions very simply. Your soul gifts support your most *natural* expression of *love.* Through these, you express the love that you are, and these gifts allow you to experience the love of others as it is reflected back to you through the receiving of your gifts.

The answer is so straightforward and yet so profound. Stripping away the monetary aspects of why we work, the phrase, "Follow your heart and the money will come" suddenly makes so much sense. You are here to express the love you are, using the gifts that give you immense joy. Your joy becomes the joy of another. Love begets love, so to speak.

The spirit world speaks in visions and symbols dancing on feelings that flow through my body. With these answers above came a vision with other examples to further explain this simple idea.

In this vision, I saw a woman who is an amazing dancer and choreographer. She is passionate, heart-full and spirit-led. I saw her dancing in my mind's eye and I heard the Messengers say, "This is how she *is* love. Do you see how she *dances* love? How she moves love around her? See this love go out and touch others. See how they give the love back to her."

Another person came into my vision. This time, it was a prolific author I love to read. He had many, many books all around him. He had written some of them; while others were from other authors he enjoyed reading. I could feel his love of books surrounding him.

"Do you see how he infuses love into his *writing*? His love is expressed through this primary soul gift of writing. He *becomes* love when he writes. He is one with love in this state. Can you sense how his books hold this love?" As I took this vision in, I could easily understand this concept of *being* love. I have read several of his books, and they do feel this way to me. I love being in their energy–they feel expansive, like anything is possible.

Then the invitation came…

Will you express the love you are?
Will you love others through your gifts?
Will you share yourself with them?
They are seeking you as much as you are seeking them.
Will you be the love you are?

Your Invitation

I share this beautiful invitation with you as well. Will you be the love that you are? Will you put down the burden you bear of all that you are not? Is it time to let go of proving so you can start living?

One morning a Messenger talked about what people are truly searching for. He said it is the divine connection that tells them everything is okay–that they are always safe, and that they are always cared for–*no matter what*. Living a *True You* life is about understanding that your life *is* your gift, no matter how bad it may look (or feel), because you are connected to the love you were created from in *every moment*. In the present, that love is *always* available to you.

In essence, you can never be away from what you are–the love that is always flowing to you surrounds you even if your heart is not open to receive it. It is an open invitation available at any time.

A *True You* life is not about *making* your life true and then living it, it is about realizing it is *already* true and enjoying it. What you are seeking is already within you and is seeking you. The divine connection you yearn for, the feeling of connection, is *you*–fully expressed as the divinity that created you.

When we are seeking this connection to the ultimate love–and the love we are, we look for it in things (material wealth and otherwise), we look for it in entertainment, we look for it in food, drugs, drink and anything else we can try to fill the void. The problem with that is that the void will only be filled by that which truly comforts the soul, and that is the love of the Creator moving through the love you are.

For years, Gayle Zinda (*www.GayleZinda.com*) took care of cancer patients. One by one, year after year, as the owner of Image Insights, a company dedicated to fitting wigs and sharing messages of faith and hope through pampering women with cancer, Gayle would take women who looked like POWs and turn them back into graceful swans. Using her cosmetic wizardry, wigs and prosthetics, Gayle transformed women into a semblance of their former selves.

Over time, Gayle came to find that the women, the many volunteers and the people who supported her business didn't necessarily come for her cosmetology talents. They came for the love she expressed in each fitting. They came for a dose of compassion and a boost from her giving heart. She shared the love she is by serving people in need. If there was ever a need, Gayle would certainly be there.

Gayle became the owner of this wonderful business by responding to the call of another person who shared that same way of expressing love. In her book, *Pink Lemonade,* Gayle shares the story of Rita Snider, a woman dying of cancer, who selected Gayle to take over her business after asking God to send the 'right person.' Gayle was no more looking for a business than she was looking to compete for Miss America, but the love she expressed was a match for the love Rita expressed, and the rest, as they say, is history.

Now it's your turn.

Will you share your soul with the world? Will you dance and make us smile? Will you create your art so we can share in your vision? Will you care for your children and be the mother or father you dreamed about being as a child? Will you smile at the cashier at the grocery store knowing that you are powerful beyond measure and reflect that power back to the person handing you your change?

I hope so, because what I know for sure is that you *do* matter and you have a special purpose here. Even the ocean knows when a thimble of water is gone…the same goes for the love you are. Shine brightly for all to see and help others see their light along the way.

Love, big hugs and peace to you-

Tina Ferguson, a.k.a. The Queen of Dreams

Three Life-altering Questions

"I'm so sick and tired of doing this over and over again. I'm sick of it!" she lamented. "Do you even understand what I've been through? I've done this over and over again and I'm sick to death of ending up in this same spot."

I sat quietly on the other end of the phone. She was exactly right. She was in a cycle of enough, not enough, enough and not enough again. The indecisive energy that brought her to this moment in time was pushing her to make another choice. It was time to do something different.

"I do understand," I ventured. "I've even done what you are doing now myself. My question for you is, 'Is it time to do something different?'"

The question was met with silence. I could almost hear silent tears falling. I don't remember what I thought next. I opened my mouth and said, "You know you aren't alone, don't you? There isn't a person on this planet that has not been right where you are now."

"Really?" came the startled response muffled through choked up tears. "You mean I'm not the only one who has made a mess of everything?"

She was a tender soul with a heart of gold. A nurturing caretaker, Maria, had a habit of taking care of everyone else instead of addressing her own needs. When she felt scared, she would adopt another stray pet to keep herself occupied. Her long list of stray pets included an ex-husband, several friends, a mother, a sister, a husband and a series of business projects. I enjoyed working with this smart young woman who could easily tune into her own energy and identify her corresponding thoughts of how she was feeling.

As she asked the question, I could see her inner child. She was peeking out from behind a skirt. She wanted to go out to play, but stayed put because she was 'bad.'

"Yes, we all have our messes. Some of us are slow learners, some fast, we all have messes, but what we don't always understand is that every mess is perfect," I replied. "Maria, I know you are upset about this lack of momentum in your life. And I know that most things seem to cost something, but if there was something you could do right now and money wasn't an object, what would you do?"

"Roller skate," she said in less than 10 seconds flat.

"That is great. Go do that. Go roller skate and let's talk tomorrow," I urged her.

"But I can't do that," she protested. "I've got to clean up this mess. I've got to figure out how to fix this big mess I'm in."

"Nothing is going to happen until you free up some resources and space so you can create something new," I offered. "Taking an hour or two out to roller skate is what you need to get to your answers. This is you talking to you. It's what you want right now. I don't want to roller skate. Does your husband want to roller skate?"

"No," she said half-heartedly.

"Well, there is a reason you want to roller skate right now," I declared.

"I don't know," she said, doubting her inner wisdom. "I have no idea why I even said that now that I'm thinking about it."

What Maria didn't know is that the inner child is the place inside of us that holds our creativity. The inner child is the *dreamer.* When we need solutions, especially fast solutions, it's the inner child who can help us. If, like Maria, we are locking up our inner child because she has done something 'bad,' then that part of us can't come out, play and create with our conscious being.

"Go roller skate. Call me tomorrow, I'm hanging up now. And I want you to smile and have fun for me, too!" I said as I hung up the phone.

The next day Maria called. "You are never going to believe what happened," she exclaimed. "It was like a bolt of lightning hit me on the way to the roller rink. I was driving there, thinking this is the most ridiculous thing I've ever done, I don't even know why I'm doing this. What is the point? I can't even afford to do this!"

"Yes and…"

"Well, as I rounded the curve to get to the rink, I couldn't believe my eyes," she said excitedly. "I saw that the rink was almost completely empty. I thought earlier that I didn't want to go because I knew that there would be a bunch of kids there and that I would feel self-conscious and, well, you know what I mean."

Smiling to myself as I tracked along with the images, enjoying the energy of her reliving the experience, I urged her to go on.

"So I almost turned around to leave, and then something told me to go in so I did," she said. "You will never believe what happened next."

I expect and delight in the words, "you'll never believe," and to this day, I am still in a constant state of awe of how we are always supported in our journeys. I never know what will happen with people, I just know something *always* happens if they trust themselves and God.

"I went in and the owner said that the rink was under its annual maintenance. He told me that the week before they cleaned the rink and this week they were painting and doing maintenance around the inside. He invited me to come skate by myself!"

With this, I could feel the joy in her being and I could see her inner child dancing around and celebrating.

"I went in and what happened is something I will never forget. I got my skates–and he didn't even charge me! I put them on and I started skating around. Slowly at first, then a little faster, then more and then soon I was moving around the rink. I felt like I was flying–kind of floating and then I put my arms out and closed my eyes and then I heard the music come on. He put on *Dancing Queen* by ABBA for me to skate to! That was one of my favorites when I was a kid!"

"Then what happened?" I asked.

"I started dancing with my roller skates and I felt as if I was in water just floating over the floor. It was like my legs weren't even connected to the floor…my entire body felt like every cell in it was alive.

I knew in that moment that *I am ready. I am worth it.* I am totally worth all that I really want in my life."

I could hear the pitch of her voice drop as she announced this aloud.

"Can you say that again?" I asked. "I can barely hear you."

"I said I am worth it. I am ready," she said only slightly louder.

"If that's your Truth, let's hear it from your soul," I urged.

"I am READY! I am worth doing something different! I know I can do it!" she proclaimed with a giggle.

"Great, let's get moving," I agreed. I could see her inner child jumping up and down, excited and very happy.

Not long after that, Maria's life took a rapid change. Friends that seemed to always see the worst in her dropped out of sight. Her husband reflected her decisiveness and started getting his life in order, too. Her coaching business took off and she soon had more clients than she ever expected. The "mess" that delivered her to this slice of living also resolved itself easily.

Is it time for you to do something different?

Are you worth it?

Are you ready?

If so, let's go!

Notes

"Dream lofty dreams
and as you dream, so shall you become."
-James Allen

Notes

"If you follow your bliss, you put yourself on a kind of track that has been there all the while, waiting for you, and the life that you ought to be living is the one you are living. When you can see that, you begin to meet people who are in your field of bliss, and they open doors to you. I say, follow your bliss and don't be afraid, and doors will open where you didn't know they were going to be."

-Joseph Campbell

Notes

"It may be true that the unexamined life is not worth living—but neither is the unlived life worth examining."

-Dan Millman

Notes

"You must live in the present,
launch yourself on every
wave, find your eternity in
each moment."
-Henry David Thoreau

Notes

"The fool, with all his other faults, has this also, he is always getting ready to live."

-Epicurus

Notes

"A warrior must cultivate the feeling that he has everything needed for the extravagant journey that is his life. What counts for a warrior is being alive. Life in itself is sufficient, self-explanatory and complete. Therefore, one may say without being presumptuous that the experience of experiences is being alive."

-Carlos Casteneda

Notes

"If we agree that the
bottom line of life
is happiness,
not success,
then it makes
perfect sense
to say that it is
the journey
that counts,
not reaching
the destination."
-Mihaly Csikszentmihalyi

Notes

"Somewhere along the line of development we discover what we really are and then make our real decision for which we are responsible. Make that decision primarily for yourself because you can never really live anyone else's life, not even your child's. The influence you exert is through your own life and what you become yourself."

-Eleanor Roosevelt

Bibliography & Thank You

Chuck Brodsky

www.ChuckBrodsky.com

We Are Each Others Angels Lyrics

From the Album: A Fingerpainter's Murals

Page 150

Gayle Zinda

www.GayleZinda.com

Pink Lemonade

Page 182

Sara Hickman

Official State Musician of Texas

www.SaraHickman.com

We Are Each Others Angels Lyrics

From the Album: Spiritual Appliances

Page 205

Toolkit Index

Self-love Tools That Can Support You to Feel Good Fast

Clarity Creatin' Tools That Show You What is True for You

Connecting to Divine: Tools to Use to Tap In to God

Questions That Connect You to You

In Case of Ditch Emergency, Use This!

If you are deep in the ditch and desire a quick route to the *feeling* that things *will be okay,* use this quick toolkit to quickly reconnect to the *True You* and God.

Step 1 – Make a decision to return to yourself and reconnect with love (the *True You).*

Step 2– Next, identify a time when you felt great, where things were going your way and life felt like it was easy. Remember this moment and allow the *feeling* of it to bathe your tired soul in love. This will be your Vision Point until you start feeling good again. For just the next few days, if you start to feel bad, down, hopeless or any other low level feeling, just stop and take a moment to remember this time and spend a few minutes in the *feelings* of the *True You.* Then, just start again...you will find that your actions, your ideas and your language follow this knowing of yourself.

Step 3 – Now, *Sort Fact From Fiction.* In this step, you will create a list of what is on your mind right now. List everything you are fearful of, worried about, concerned about and afraid might actually happen as a result of your current situation. Next to each item, write out the Truth so you can dismantle the fiction. Use another sheet of paper if you have more fiction. Better outside of you than inside of you!

Fiction (Thoughts I'm Currently Having)	Fact (The Truth of the Situation)
Ex: *I don't have enough money for rent. I'm afraid I will get kicked out of my apartment.*	Ex: *Rent is not due for two more weeks. I have 14 days for something to change.*

Step 4 – Now, reconnect to that time when you felt great–where all the lights were green and the world was safe and a wonderful place to live.

Step 5 - Decide what you most want. Or, simply hand it over to God to decide what is best for you. Either way, ask for the best step for you to now take. Here's a simple way to ask:

Dear God,

I'm not even sure what to pray for. Please put love in my heart and action in my feet to move toward what is best for me right now.

Thank you. Amen.

Trust the first thing that pops in your mind. It may not look anything like what you *think* you need. Go with whatever comes to you.

Step 6 – For the next few days, just mind your feelings and return to your *good feelings* (by remembering your Vision Point, which is simply how you want to *feel* right now) whenever you find yourself slipping back toward the ditch. Once you reconnect, then ask for a next step and take it.

Within a few days, you'll be feeling like the old you again–the *True You.*

A Message from The Ferguson Family

You are divine and beautiful just as you are. You are special beyond your wildest imagination. Every day that you rise with your heart open to meet the adventure that is your life you are a testament to God's love. Your personal journey in this life is unique and makes a beautiful mark on the world and the lives around you *even though you may not see it.* If you ever feel isolated, please know that you are never alone in this life even when things might not look their best because you will always have our family out in the world with you, loving you and holding a space for your dreams and your *True You*. Let the true person that is inside of you be free. The person who is wanting to play, to explore, to share, to love, and to remember the joy that is available to you each and every day is *already* who you are–*today*!

Love,

Tina, Mark, Chance & Rico ♥

We love to hear from you.

Send letters to:

Tina Ferguson International, P.O. Box 864093, Plano, Texas 75086

Email letters to: letters@TinaFerguson.com

About the Author

Tina Ferguson, a.k.a. The Queen of Dreams

Tina Ferguson is a visionary catalyst and CEO of Tina Ferguson International, a company dedicated to supporting people from all walks of life to accelerate inner mastery, and access to the divine, abundance and personal power. She is an award-winning author, intuitive strategist, artist and life catalyst who enjoys playing big and encourages others to play big, too. Known as The Queen of Dreams, Tina's greatest joy is assisting others in making their wildest dreams come true. She is a popular and top-rated public speaker and is also the Host of the Queen of Dreams Show, which airs each Thursday night around the world. She is the creator and author of ***The Power of Love, The Power of Love Meditations, Must Be Present To Win: How To Get Out Of The Ditch and Plug Back In To Your Passion*** and ***The Marketing Multiplier Effect: Making Money is SO Easy...You Can Do This Too!*** She lives in Plano, Texas with her with her husband, Mark; son, Chance and 190 lb. bundle of canine love, Rico.

Learn more at
www.TinaFerguson.com

Tina Ferguson, a.k.a. The Queen of Dreams

Tina Speaks! Go to www.TinaFerguson.com/speaking for more information.

Give me 90 minutes and I'll assist you to reconnect with your purpose!

If you've tried everyone else's way, now is the time to find your way to live on purpose, in passion and with more abundance than ever before.

Discover the True You and your unique way to be the love you are.

Soul Gifts

True Passion True You True Talents

Soul Path

Call 469-777-8336 for a True You Session today!

Join others, just like you, who are creating their juicy dreams & lives!

* **Free Downloads** – Get free downloads for this book and more.
* **Free Newsletter** – Subscribe to Tina's In-Powered Living newsletter and get a special gift from the Queen of Dreams.
* **Dream Forum** – Join others who are creating their own dreams!
* **Tina's Blog** – Every week, Tina share's new insights for living your best *True You* life.
* **Queen of Dreams Radio** – Download Tina's top-rated, weekly show for a hit of inspiration. Access a vast library of shows, too.
* **Workshops & Retreats** – Learn more about attending a Queen of Dreams event near you.
* **Services** – Discover more about working personally with Tina.

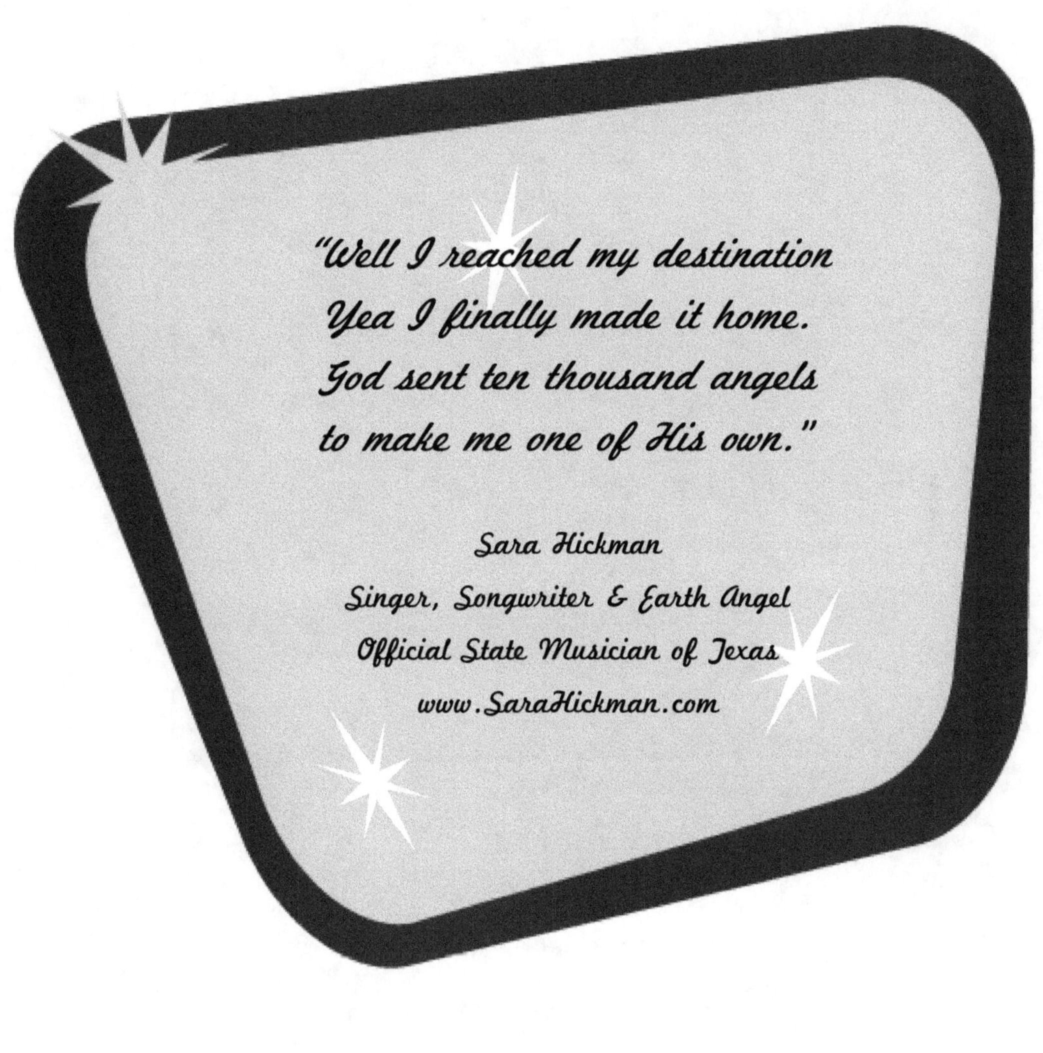
"Well I reached my destination
Yea I finally made it home.
God sent ten thousand angels
to make me one of His own."
Sara Hickman
Singer, Songwriter & Earth Angel
Official State Musician of Texas
www.SaraHickman.com

www.ingramcontent.com/pod-product-compliance
Lightning Source LLC
LaVergne TN
LVHW061221100826
845148LV00004B/820
* 9 7 8 0 9 8 1 7 3 9 0 1 4 *